ASSERT

C000226848

COMMUNICATION

The Complete Guide to Communicating Assertively and Awarely, Expressing Yourself Authoritatively, Building Self-Esteem

ROBERTO VINGELLI

DEDICATION

I dedicate this book to those of you, who at this moment, reside in the darkness of your consciousness, in fear or in the uncertainty of the future.

To you I say...STRENGTH!!! Don't give up! Take it one step at a time...one round at a time and remember, whatever event knocks you down... ALWAYS GET UP!!!

The adversity and the hard times have served to fortify you, provide clarity and illuminate your new path.
They were simply the training before the battle, the preparation for new challenges and the signal for change.
Never doubt your ability to make it, rest at the end and never in the middle. Any failure is just a new experience, a new knowledge that enriches you and gives you wisdom.

Accept it all with strength and courage because there is indeed a different way of looking at things.

With love

Roberto Vingelli

Logos are used without the permission or support of the trademark owner and the trademark is published without the permission or support of the owner. Trademarks and logos mentioned in this book are the property of their respective owners and are not associated with this document.

Summary

I wish you an enjoyable reading and if you enjoy this book please write a review, I will be grateful.

Feel free to contact me through my socials or my website, I will reply to you personally.

Roberto Vingelli

<u>INTRODUCTION</u>

We as people tend to argue a lot, but if we used assertive communication skills, those conversations would make a huge difference in how our relationships proceed.

Assertive communication skills begin in the mind, with a thought or commitment to using them.

Engagement revolves around "I-phrases," experiencing consciousness, calming the heartbeat, playfulness, reflective listening, and providing options.

The purpose in using reflective listening is to teach assertive communication skills with examples. When I ask clients how they feel when someone is paying attention to them, the typical response is "good."

In fact, I can see an irritated person calming down immediately when I use reflective listening skills.

Understanding the assertive approach will also help you deal more effectively with family members, colleagues and co-workers, reducing drama and stress. Finally, being assertive allows you to draw the necessary lines in relationships, allowing you to meet your own needs without alienating others or allowing distrust and anger to creep into your life.

This allows you to get what you need in relationships while satisfying the desires of your loved ones. Many people associate assertive speech with tension and hostility, but assertiveness often brings people closer together.

Assertive communication is a skill that needs to be honed. People often confuse assertiveness with aggression, but assertiveness is really a quiet middle ground between aggression and passivity. Aggression causes sad feelings and broken bonds. Passivity breeds fatigue, anger and, in extreme cases, outbursts.

CHAPTER 1

WHAT IS MEANT BY ASSERTIVENESS

Assertiveness is a trait often mentioned when teaching social and communication skills.

Being assertive requires being able to advocate for your own or others' interests in a respectful and calm manner, without being abusive or passive.

Individuals who are assertive are able to express their points without offending people or being offended themselves.

Although everyone behaves passively and aggressively from time to time, these attitudes are often the product of a lack of self-confidence. As a result, they are unacceptable ways of communicating with others.

According to the Concise Oxford Dictionary, assertiveness is defined as:

"Outspoken and constructive insistence on respect for one's rights."

In other words, assertiveness involves standing up for one's personal rights and sharing opinions, emotions, and values in a direct, truthful, and acceptable manner.

Therefore, it is important to remember that by being assertive, we must still value the opinions, emotions, and values of others.

Those who act assertively often value the opinions, emotions, and values of others in addition to their own.

Assertiveness is a personal, organizational and essential skill that involves the ability to adequately articulate thoughts, needs, desires and requests. Assertiveness can help you put yourself forward in a simple, transparent, and rational manner in all of your relationships, both personal and professional.

Assertive individuals are willing to act in their own best interest. They are able to stand up for themselves without becoming anxious, as well as share true emotions without denying the rights of others.

An assertion is a safe mode of communication. It is an opportunity to defend ourselves in a frank and polite manner. Every day we see circumstances in which being assertive can be helpful, such as asking someone for an appointment, confronting a teacher with a question, or doing well in a professional or college interview.

Being assertive is not something everyone is born with. Some people communicate in an overly passive manner. Others have an overly defensive demeanor. The comfortable balance between these two is an assertive style.

That's what it means to be assertive:
- You can offer your ideas and suggestions.
- You can say no without feeling guilty.
- You can give an opinion or say how you feel.
- You can ask for what you want or need.
- You can respectfully disagree.

Assertiveness involves being assertive enough to defend one's own interests, as well as those of others, in a cool, direct, and constructive manner without being unnecessarily offensive.

This skill allows us to interact effectively or express our thoughts and sorrows while keeping calm. It can be found in all communication and social skills training courses as a topic. Assertiveness does not imply or promise victory in all cases. When assertiveness is displayed, the interests and legitimacy of others should also be considered. An individual with strong assertiveness skills is someone who can reconcile their own desires with the desires and rights of opposing parties.

THE IMPORTANCE OF ASSERTIVENESS.

Assertiveness has several benefits. There will be times in your career when bosses, elected officials, the public and others will betray you. In such situations, assertiveness is more than just a useful tool. It is one of the most effective ways to deal with wrong attitudes without causing upheaval in work environments.

Assertiveness also has the following benefits:

- Implements self-esteem. Assertiveness and self-confidence are directly related. Practicing assertiveness automatically increases the rate of confidence.
- Relieves Stress. Assertiveness allows you to express your emotions, make your voice heard, and resolve your dilemma while remaining calm. This removes unresolved emotions and inner sadness that cause depression and anger.
- Prevents or reduces conflict. Excellent assertiveness skills eliminate or reduce the likelihood of becoming a troublemaker in the company.

CHAPTER 2
A PRACTICAL TEST TO MEASURE YOUR ASSERTIVENESS

Are you a human doormat? Do you always say "yes" when in truth you mean "no"? Do you keep your thoughts to yourself for fear of offending or provoking others?

With this test you will see if you defend yourself in the best possible way.

The ability to express and articulate your ideas, beliefs, and desires in a simple, concise, and non-aggressive manner is called assertiveness. This assessment decides whether a lack of assertiveness skills is preventing you from reaching your full potential and achieving your goals. Consider the following points and indicate how often or to what extent you agree with them.

Some people are more assertive by nature than others. However, if you're not one of these alpha type characters, you may feel like you've been crushed. Being assertive is difficult for many people, but it's important to make sure your message is heard loud and clear at all times. At the same time, you don't want to come across as pushy, overbearing, or offensive.

Spend a few moments considering what you would most likely say or do in the following situations:

1. YOU PROPOSE A SOLUTION TO A PROBLEM IN A CONFERENCE IN YOUR DEPARTMENT, BUT A COLLEAGUE INTERRUPTS YOU BEFORE YOU CAN FINISH.

a) You tap your hand on the table, look your colleague in the eye, and start talking louder and louder.
b) You stop, lean back, and let your colleague continue the conversation.
c) Listen to the interruption and send the colleague a hand gesture to say, "One minute." Continue and ask for feedback from the colleague when you're done.

2. *YOUR BOSS GRANTS YOU WRITTEN LEAVE FOR FRIDAY, BUT ON THURSDAY NIGHT HE INFORMS YOU THAT THE DEPARTMENT IS RUNNING LATE AND YOU MUST REPORT TO WORK ON FRIDAY.*

a) (Arms crossed over your chest) "I'm not okay with this. You said I could take time off. Why don't you do that with the whole night group? Why am I yelled at just because I work during the day?"
b) "I thought you said you didn't need me? I'll be there."
c) "That sounds important. You know I'm committed to keeping this department active, but I have important plans for tomorrow. I could stay late tonight or work over the weekend instead."

3. *A COLLEAGUE TAKES CREDIT FOR AN IDEA YOU COME UP WITH DURING A MEETING.*

a) You don't talk much, but you're looking for a way to copy one of his ideas to make him look ridiculous. You become angry, even furious!
b) You say nothing to anyone and spend the next few days upset, scolding yourself for being stupid and exploited.

c) You go to him and say, "I'm having a hard time trusting you as you present my proposals to our leader as if they were your own. I confided my ideas to you and you betrayed my trust."

4. *IN ORDER FOR YOU TO BE MORE SUCCESSFUL IN YOUR CURRENT JOB, YOU ARE PROMISED A LARGER ROOM IN YOUR NEW OFFICE. WHEN YOU WALK IN, HOWEVER, YOU ARE TOLD, "SORRY, IT DIDN'T WORK OUT THE WAY WE EXPECTED."*

a) You slam your drawers and yell at your fellow neighbors before moving. Every time something changes, you sarcastically associate it with the broken pledge.
b) You shrug and silently mull over your decision.
c) You recognize that improvements are inevitable with a transition of this magnitude, and you inform the responsible party that you may need more space to efficiently represent your clients and colleagues. You have several options and are open to new ideas.

Ask yourself the following questions for each "A" answer you gave:

- What do I think I need to prove?
- How do I expect other people to "pay" for what happened?
- What will be the result of my behaviors?
- What can I lose if I react this way?

Ask yourself the following questions about each "B" answer you gave:
- What am I afraid of?
- What will be the consequences of my answer?
- What can I lose by responding like this?

For every "C" answer, ask yourself:
- Why did I choose this answer?
- What will be the outcome of my response?
- What can I gain from this response?

To be successful in today's fast-paced environment, you must be able to communicate effectively. However, if you are not consciously expressing your desires, thoughts, and points of view, it is possible to get lost in the shuffle. By spending some time considering how you react to different circumstances, you will project yourself as a more assertive person. Soon you'll be thinking more confidently, releasing tension and convincing people of your point of view.

HOW TO IMPROVE ASSERTIVENESS

One skill that many people lack is the ability to properly express their displeasure in the most appropriate way. The following tips will help you become a better communicator:

COMMUNICATE THE DILEMMA IN DETAIL

You should be clear in your requests and respond accordingly. Avoid complaining about insignificant things or prevaricating. Secondly, deal with the most relevant or crucial issues.

ATTACK THE PROBLEM, NOT THE PEOPLE:

Keep in mind that an assertive individual is not a source of misunderstanding. Do not criticize people's personalities or say they are prejudiced or unfair to you. Rather, illustrate why you feel it is a bad decision, an accusation, or a threat to jeopardize your rights or privileges. Convince them why you feel they made an unintentional mistake rather than an effort to discredit you.

BE CONFIDENT

This is especially important when working with people who have made a deliberate attempt to subjugate you because they believe you are ignorant. Your boldness in conveying your demands demonstrates your seriousness.

KNOW YOUR RIGHTS AND OBLIGATIONS

You cannot be assertive if you do not know what your rights, limitations, and privileges are. Once you have a thorough understanding of your rights, freedoms, and limitations, you will be able to speak with clarity and gain confidence through available evidence to support your arguments.

WHY LEARN TO BE ASSERTIVE

Individuals who are assertive experience fewer disagreements with others, which results in less tension in their lives. This often causes more trusting relationships.

Passive personalities escape confrontation by failing to communicate their desires and emotions. These behaviors will destroy relationships over time. They will feel victimized and discourage conflict. Before the initially calm person explodes, the other party doesn't know there's a problem. Aggression, on the other hand, will alienate others and cause undue tension. Those who are targets of abusive behavior will feel attacked and may avoid the aggressive person.

CHAPTER 3
WHAT IS ASSERTIVE COMMUNICATION

The ability to convey positive and negative ideas and feelings freely, truthfully, and directly is called assertive communication. It acknowledges our rights but continues to acknowledge the rights of others. It allows us to accept responsibility for our decisions without judging or blaming others. It allows us to deal with disagreement constructively and find a mutually satisfactory solution.

Assertive communication involves direct and truthful statements about one's values, needs, and emotions.
When interacting assertively, you should express your thoughts without judging those of others. You speak for yourself whenever possible, and you do so in a polite and thoughtful manner because assertiveness involves respect for your ideas and those of others.
This approach to communication is very effective in resolving conflicts collaboratively.
Whether you have a serious problem you wish to share with your partner or simply need to inform a colleague that you are unable to help them with a job, assertive dialogue helps you communicate your wishes productively and work with the other party to find an answer.

Although it may be uncomfortable, assertiveness is a leadership style that has been linked to a wide range of positive outcomes in a variety of areas.
The ability to communicate and engage in a way that understands and respects the interests and viewpoints of

others while still standing up for one's own personal rights, needs, and boundaries is known as assertive communication. Assertiveness is a powerful, non-confrontational means of communicating one's dissatisfaction with a given circumstance or idea.

Maria Daniela Pipas and Mohammad Jaradat (2010) stated that assertive communicators should speak about their own (or others') interests in a frank and graceful manner, reducing interpersonal tensions and maintaining respect for others.

Assertiveness can include refusing requests ("No, I won't lend you any more money."); initiating, maintaining, or ending a dialogue ("I would like to negotiate my reward with you."); asking for favors ("Would you kindly help me change the tire?"); and expressing positive and negative emotions ("You hurt me when you talk to me like that.")

Overall, while assertive communication takes many forms and occurs in a variety of contexts, it usually involves pursuing one's goals without causing awkward scenarios or risking relationships.

The following scenarios will help you get a better view:

WITH A FRIEND

Your roommate has a crush on one of your close friends and seems to be interested. When you make arrangements to stay with one of them, they ask if the other will be there (which you find a little annoying).
You've had some bad luck with the roommates and friends you've been hanging out with and you're worried about how this will turn out. You also know that your roommate is not interested in a serious relationship, while your friend is emphatically so.

One day, your friend says, "Would it be okay if I asked your roommate out?"
Taking courage, you say:
"I am concerned that this will impact our friendship, especially if your relationship doesn't work out. This has happened to me before, complicated my living conditions, and led to the loss of a close friend. Also, my roommate prefers something less serious."

THE RESULT

Your friend is dissatisfied but not furious. In fact, you both accept that you don't want to jeopardize your friendship and understand that the situation could get complicated.

AT WORK

Your boss has pitched you a big upcoming project several times, stating that he wants you to focus on it because it targets clients you've already dealt with.

"It would be perfect to add to your portfolio when you're preparing for promotion," they say. "You're more than prepared for it."

Your heart is filled with happiness as they deliver the supplies for the project and the due date. You have some critical business that you can't put off because there's no way you can get it done on your own.

At the same time, you don't want to disappoint your employer or your clients because you really want the raise.

You call your manager to try to justify: "I want to prioritize this project, but I'm afraid that if I undertake it, all my work will suffer. I'd like to show you what I'm capable of with this, but I need to be able to do my best."

THE RESULT

Your manager agrees that you have too much on your mind. You decide together that one of the heaviest tasks should be delegated to someone else, freeing you to manage the new project.

WITH A PARTNER

You have started a serious relationship with someone. Even though you adore him and love spending time with him, there's a problem. He's too messy.
You always see dishes in the sink and laundry on the floor. The floor is rarely washed and the bathroom is almost always in disarray.

So far, you've sent him a few hints but haven't said anything directly. Rather, you decide to simply receive him at your home because you feel more comfortable in your (clean) bedroom.

"Why don't you like to visit me?" your partner asks you one day.

You don't want to offend but you still want to be honest, so you say:

I get overwhelmed when I'm in a cluttered environment and it takes my attention away from enjoying your company. Would you mind doing the dishes, laundry, and cleaning up a bit before I come over? It would make me feel more comfortable.

THE RESULT

Your partner doesn't feel judged or like you're asking them to change. They want you to feel comfortable and agree to tidy up a bit.

DEALING WITH BULLIES

Bullying tends to have long-term negative effects on many young people. Assertive negotiation is a valuable skill to prevent such actions from happening.

Anti-bullying initiatives such as Problem-Based Learning (PBL) have been introduced in schools (Hall, 2005). PBL, in combination with teacher and parent engagement, teaches children assertiveness skills. This therapeutic approach assists adolescents in developing action plans and practicing techniques to minimize aggressive abuse, name-calling, and the spreading of gossip.

PBL has been shown to improve problem solving skills in youth (Hall, 2005). These skills should also be used to teach children that bullying is not appropriate behavior for anyone. For example, children with assertive problem solving skills are better able to advocate for a targeted child, inviting them to participate in their programs and by informing an instructor of what is happening.

WHY IT'S WORTH IT

Arguing is not an issue for assertive individuals. Comments are not offensive and are often unquestionable. "I-phrases" that begin with "I feel..., I would like to..., I am concerned about..." are indisputable and no one can argue against you "feeling" or "thinking" a certain way.
These "I-phrases" are great dialogue cues because they get you to stop blaming the other party and it encourages them to save face or take responsibility before getting emotional. If

you are used to arguing with someone and attempting to use this method for the first time, you may see an immediate change in the conversation. Continue to use "I-phrases" if the other person becomes abusive or passive. *"I will not resume this discussion until we all agree on that particular thing,"* for example. For the more passive person, *"I understand that you're not ready to talk to me and I appreciate that, and I know I can't make you. When you decide you are, I'll be ready."*

Keep in mind that you do not have to agree. You will show confidence if you say, *"I disagree."* If you are stumped on a particular topic, the most assertive response is to say, *"I'll have to get back to you on that later."* This is an excellent statement for those who find it difficult to say no. It gives you time to consider the conditions you will accept if you say yes.

Sometimes my clients ask me, *"What if someone hits you, since you can't get free, you have no choice but to be aggressive?"* *"Assertively hit them and retreat,"* I reply. What I really mean is that assertiveness, by definition, involves expressing your goal correctly and effectively. If you are being exploited and have no means of getting out of the situation, your intention should be to defend yourself. Do just that and leave as soon as possible. You are not being violent in this way; you are just protecting yourself and setting boundaries.
However, I have found that with experience, verbal assertiveness is more useful and almost always prevents escalation even if it requires more time and control than offensive communication.

HERE ARE SOME OF THE KEY BENEFITS OF PASSIVE CONTACT FOR YOU AND YOUR RELATIONSHIPS:

PROTECTS YOUR NEEDS

- You have the opportunity to put stakes in issues that you don't feel like addressing politely.
- You can distinctly communicate emotions and use those feelings to set boundaries in any relationship by speaking assertively.
- Respect your desires as you make decisions about yourself, about what you can and won't do.
- Having strong boundaries and remembering them out of necessity allows you to assert yourself in potentially difficult circumstances and decreases feelings of anger and dissatisfaction.

BUILDS TRUST

- If integrity is the right policy to adopt, then assertive contact is the way to go. People are more likely to believe you if they know you can have clear and transparent answers.
- White lies or lies by omission are often the result of passive contact. Even if you're not directly misleading, unintentional ambiguity can be damaging.
- People may get the impression that you are not telling them anything they can trust if you hide behind situations to avoid confrontation and your opinions.
- Aggressive contact can frighten or alienate others, eroding trust, even deceptively.

PREVENTS STRESS

Consider the example we saw earlier of relationships at work. Instead of passively promising to work on additional projects, you expressed your concerns about your current workload. You may have been able to complete it with great satisfaction, but not without a lot of tension.

Passive behavior prevents you from expressing your desires and staying within your boundaries. Over time, this naturally leads to fatigue, anger, frustration and even exhaustion.

HELPS PREVENT CONFLICT

- What if you responded aggressively to the friend who tried to date your roommate? "No way. You can't date him. That would be bad for me."
- They would blame you for telling them what to do and the resulting tension would put a strain on the friendship.
- A passive response, such as "Okay, whatever. I don't care," can avoid confrontation in the moment. However, if your relationship is suffering because of them, your anger will escalate until it explodes into open conflict.
- Annoyance (both toward them and yourself for not speaking up) often manifests itself in passive-aggressive attitudes, such as closing the door when you see your friend and roommate together or making rude comments.
- Honesty in expressing your point of view helps avoid both of these potentially negative situations.

PROMOTES TRUST AND HEALTHY RELATIONSHIPS

- Communicating assertively will increase your self-esteem and improve the well-being of the relationship.
- When you feel comfortable expressing yourself, you are more likely to establish relationships with people who value your desires and are comfortable sharing their feelings.

CHAPTER 4
PASSIVITY, AGGRESSIVENESS, ASSERTIVENESS

Do you find it difficult to communicate with your partner in a constructive and productive way? Because we all have different characteristics and viewpoints, it can be difficult to learn healthy styles of connecting with others. A variety of variables affect the way we communicate with others. One of the most critical aspects to consider is speaking style. There are four ways of relating that need to be considered. By the end of this chapter you will have a basic understanding of the four modes of contact: active, passive, passive-aggressive, and assertive. From now on you will be able to distinguish where you use one of the four modes. All communication types have their own time and location, and it's up to you to choose when each is most appropriate for use.

AGGRESSIVE COMMUNICATION STYLE

When you have an aggressive communication style, you express your interests in a way that leaves no room for the people involved and their desires. Aggression usually stems from a sense of vulnerability. When you feel threatened, or as if your best interests are in danger, you will adopt an aggressive communication style.
Aggressive people may appear verbally abusive to others.
Since their aggressiveness stimulates the fight-or-flight instinct of the interlocutor, aggressive people may fail to interact with others.

HERE ARE SOME EXAMPLES OF AGGRESSIVE -OFFENSIVE COMMUNICATION:

- Attempts to dominate
- Frequent interruptions
- Speaking loudly and in an overbearing tone
- Criticizing others
- Using humiliation to control others
- "You-phrases"
- Easily triggered temperament

People who use an aggressive communication style may isolate themselves from others, increasing their insecurity and instilling fear or hatred in others. Aggressive people also refuse to accept responsibility for their actions because they don't want to face their insecurities, making it impossible to learn from circumstances and get the guidance and affection they crave from others.

In certain situations, using an aggressive communication approach can be beneficial. If you are feeling taken advantage of or want to make sure you are noticed, an assertive communication style can be helpful. For example, if you are competing for a promotion with a colleague, you may have to be competitive to get ahead. Another example, if a child is frequently harassed at school, you may need to show other students that you can control yourself and should not be teased. When you engage in physical exercise, such as at the gym or in a competition, an aggressive communication style can be helpful.

PASSIVE COMMUNICATION STYLE

Individuals with a passive listening approach do not communicate their thoughts or views to others. People choose a passive communication approach for a variety of purposes. Often it is to feel safe and afraid to engage in discourse. Often it is because they have a naturally relaxed attitude and like to get carried away.

People who use a passive communication style may be more tolerant of other people's behaviors. A passive communication style involves more compromise and allows the other person to get what they want, which may leave the person using a passive communication style dissatisfied. For example, if your partner is having a bad day, you might decide to take a passive approach to a problem you are experiencing with them. You'll reason to yourself, "Ah, no need to bother them, that'll be for tomorrow," but tomorrow will never come.

When perceiving a violent communication style, a passive person may agree when in truth they disagree or have something to say. The passive communication style often channels the fear of conflict and finds a way to avoid making the seemingly abusive communication style more threatening. For example, if your employer is unhappy, it may be in your best interest to be submissive and compliant to maintain your position.

Although using a passive contact style can sometimes be beneficial for relationships, doing so regularly can perpetuate passive habits and give a negative message to people that their interests are not as important as those of others. Continuous passive contact can contribute to dormant attitudes, which can lead to unhealthy relationships with others. An individual with a passive communication style may feel voiceless, as if they are not important or as if they are not loved by anyone.

BELOW ARE SOME INDICATORS OF UNHEALTHY PASSIVE COMMUNICATION:

- Allowing others to constantly meet their needs instead of prioritizing your own
- Avoiding conflict at all costs
- Ignoring situations that need to be handled as soon as possible
- Inability to speak for oneself
- Speaks softly or apologizes often
- Poor eye contact and narrowing body posture

When the use of a passive communication style has a detrimental effect, it can lead to a feeling of loss of control, which can be stressful. Feelings of hopelessness or depression can be created as a result. A passive communication approach makes it pointless to fight for your desires unless you are frustrated or hopeless. You learn that you are powerless, and from the outside it may look like a passive-aggressive type of communication. A passive communication style does not force one to fulfill one's desires, while an active communication style causes one to hold a grudge.

ASSERTIVE COMMUNICATION STYLE

In most cases, using an assertive communication style is the most powerful communication style. An assertive speaking style allows one to communicate one's desires and/or points of view simply and strongly without infringing on the interests of others. An assertive leadership style involves being aware of one's personal feelings and needs while being aware of the emotions and needs of others. Assertive people can empathize with others when they are aware of their own desires and seek to fulfill them.

Here are some behaviors of an assertive communication style:

- Expresses needs clearly, respectfully, and appropriately
- "I-Phrases"
- Active listener: listening without interruption and reflecting on what you have heard
- Talks calmly
- Good eye contact
- Relaxed body posture
- Feels in control
- Empathetic

An assertive communication style can be difficult to master because it requires a lot of self-control. Emotions are what make us people and can get the best of us as we communicate. Intense unmanaged feelings can contribute to unhealthy relationships with others. Practicing mindfulness can help in the development of an assertive communication style. A person with an assertive communication style normally feels in charge of his or her life and when new problems arise he or she takes full responsibility. As a result, it causes people to maintain stable marriages, mental stability and overall well-being.

The first step toward using an effective communication style is to understand when each of these types of communication is appropriate for use. Be honest with yourself and accept responsibility if you know you are not yet communicating in a healthy way. By learning about these four leadership styles, you will be able to develop your interpersonal skills and effectively lobby for your needs.

CHAPTER 5
UNDERSTAND YOUR FEARS

Fear is useful if it doesn't totally paralyze us from acting. Fear reminds us of our humanity, prevents us from walking in front of moving cars, and can cause "fight or flight" responses, allowing us to avoid getting involved in dangerous situations. However, as communicators, we need to become aware of any fear that may prevent us from communicating with others by speaking or writing.

Many people quote Franklin Delano Roosevelt's observation that *"the only thing we have to be afraid of is fear itself."* His wife Eleanor's even more realistic quote is even more fascinating: *"Do one thing every day that scares you."* The first lady argued that rather than stop and try to overcome anxiety, accept it and move on.

Even in the world of work, fears play a fundamental role, being terribly limiting for the person.

This means you can be the most educated person in any subject, but if you can't easily express your knowledge to someone, you're not worth much to most employers.
Years of studies on this subject have shown three important attributes that every employer looks for, regardless of the vacancy being filled. These attributes include verbal and written communication skills, problem-solving skills, and the ability to successfully collaborate with others.

Above all, employers want to understand a candidate's level of communication, regardless of the role he or she will be filling.

Having said that, what do you think is people's biggest fear? Numerous surveys and interviews show that the most common concern is public speaking.

However, there is only one way to overcome the terror of standing up and expressing what you think: DO IT!

Do you find it difficult to open up? Many people, whether they admit it or not, are afraid to communicate. Sometimes it can be difficult to open up to someone and express your true feelings. However, the more you stop focusing on your fear of communicating, the worse it will get.

Fear is due to self-preservation or the need for others to see you in a positive light. It can be helpful in certain situations, but most of the time it is a hindrance. Giving in to the fear of contact keeps you from expressing your reality, having authentic relationships, and living life to the fullest.

Overcoming contact anxiety can be scary at first, but it only takes a little practice. If you want to be the strongest version of yourself, you need to learn how to relate freely and effectively.

MANY PEOPLE HAVE THE SAME FEAR OF COMMUNICATION AS YOU DO

You are not alone in your fear of communication. Communication anxiety is a major problem that many people face. Parents struggle with their children, couples struggle with each other, employees struggle with co-workers, and so on.

Fear of communication is one of many almost universal human feelings. Your communication problems are not a reflection of you, but it is your duty to solve them. If you didn't solve them, you'd have a pretty hard life.

Either way, realizing that you are not alone in your battle can be helpful. You're not the only one trying to overcome your doubts.

Fears hinder our ability to meet new people, strengthen relationships, advance in our careers, and achieve financial stability. Although the internet and social media allow us to interact with thousands (and perhaps millions) of people without even saying anything, this is not necessarily the right way to achieve our goals. This is especially true when trying to alleviate the apprehension of communication.

So, what are people's communication apprehensions? The most common social phobia is definitely public speaking. Let's face it: being on stage in front of hundreds of eyes scrutinizing our every breath and expression can be intimidating.

Meeting new people is the next big social anxiety. If you're shy, you probably know the awkward feeling we get when we're in an unfamiliar environment surrounded by mysterious faces. Other social fears include asking for assistance, asking someone out, selling something, asking for a promotion, addressing a sensitive topic, getting positive feedback, and so on.

We've all been there: we're enjoying a beautiful day, and then our mood suddenly changes. Why is that? What happened? What triggered the abrupt shift from positive to negative emotion? Is there anything I can do?

These are just a few of the many thoughts that arise when we notice a change in our surroundings, a change in mood because of our partner, or a change in our partner's own mood.

Along with these questions will come the uncertainty and fear of handling such a situation. Then the real question becomes, "What do I need to do to alleviate the fear?"

In many marriages, there is a general pattern of anxiety in conversation. When something happens, a person will ask 20 questions in their head and it seems that more often than not they adopt the "play it safe" mentality. This can be for a number of reasons, including: you've recently been struggling with several stressful issues and don't want to add this latest one to the list of ones that need to be addressed; things have been going well recently and you want to continue on this path; you're trying to stop an argument; you don't want to hurt other people's feelings; you're tired of being told "what you're doing is dumb" or you tell yourself that "talking never helps." For one excuse or another, we tend to ignore these thoughts day after day, but at what cost?

Allowing these issues to escalate can have a number of negative effects on a relationship. Without realizing it, anger begins to build, suspicion enters the relationship, negative emotions increase, irritability and dissatisfaction are more easily triggered, and partners begin to drift apart. Often, one of the parties in the relationship is totally oblivious to the fact that a void is forming, convinced that they are capable of carrying all the emotional load on their own. The consequence is a buildup of anger at the other partner for not caring, supporting or remembering. Meanwhile, the other person remains trapped because they have been completely blindsided by this revelation.

Before things get worse, those almost endless questions, believe it or not, have a reason. They are there to alert you to a possible problem before it gets out of control beyond repair. This little wake-up call is there to reduce the possibility of damage to something very valuable and meaningful.

Just like when a car engine slows down making everyday life more complex, similarly communication anxiety does the same for your relationship. Yes, you'll go through the traffic light and keep driving day after day, reminding yourself that everything is perfect because your engine "seems" to be running. But there will come a time when you really need the full power of your engine and you'll start to wonder why it's not working properly.
So, how do you answer these questions without inadvertently causing the very thing we fear will happen?

SOME USEFUL TIPS TO MAKE IT EASIER

First, there is no law that requires you to address and discuss the problem as soon as it arises. Consequently, take your time. There is no need to rush. Resolute problem solving is preferable to listless problem solving.

Second, don't give in to panic. By doing so, you will be in charge rather than a victim of your emotions.

Taking the time to deal with the situation would be extremely beneficial in this case. The fear will fade over time. After reflecting, you will approach the topic with less emotion (frustration, panic, anxiety, etc.), increasing your chances of success. When one or more parties involved are emotionally charged, it is one of the most difficult times to discuss issues. Finally, be sure to approach the situation (behavior) rather than the person (your partner). We want our partner(s) to understand that the action is annoying, but not him/her as a human being. Be sure to reflect and pay attention to your strategy and speak appropriately. Otherwise, the fear will only increase. If your partner is a person with values, he/she will be able to deal with the problem more effectively, ultimately showing you that by having a healthy dialogue, there is nothing to fear.

UNDERSTAND THE SOURCE OF YOUR FEAR

In dangerous environments, the fear conservation instinct comes in handy. However, when it comes to communication fears, the situation is not particularly dangerous. Communication anxiety is also caused by the fear of being judged by the person you wish to talk to. Understanding whether your anxiety is real or unfounded will help you deal with it.

For example, you have recently started dating someone and you want to tell them something about yourself. You care about this person and want to have them by your side, but you're afraid that by exposing your vulnerability they'll pull away. Yet, any person worth having around should want to know what you're thinking.

At work you'd like to ask your boss for a raise. You're afraid they won't take you seriously, that you'll get fired, or that you'll upset the routine. Yet, the worst thing your manager could say is a simple "No". It's hard to put yourself out there, but if you don't you're only hurting yourself.

Anticipatory terror is always much greater than the actual thing you are afraid of. It is easy to understand what might or might not happen. But how many times have your worst nightmares come true?

THERE ARE TWO EXCELLENT ACRONYMS FOR FEAR

Fraudulent Testing: whether it appears to be a real or fictitious experience.

Apparent Truth: Both allude to the fact that whatever you are afraid of will most likely not become reality until it occurs.

This is also the case with contact anxiety. In your mind, you are potentially constructing a scenario that is much more daunting than it would actually be. When you talk to the person you need to talk to, you realize that it's not as bad as you thought.

STEPS TO FULLY UNDERSTAND AND OVERCOME THE FEAR OF COMMUNICATION

These basic steps are a great way to start conquering your fear and sharing what you need to communicate.

1. START SLOWLY

When it comes to overcoming your doubts, you don't have to deal with everything at once. Don't try to talk to your boss, fight with your wife, and argue with your child all in the same day. Choose the least intimidating interaction to begin with.

2. BE KIND TO YOURSELF

If you put more pressure on yourself, you would be in more trouble. Bringing yourself down for being afraid to communicate would only make it harder to engage in the necessary discussions. Be kind to yourself as you work to overcome your fear, or the path may seem even more difficult. You're more likely to continue working to overcome your fear when you treat yourself with kindness and allow yourself to make mistakes.

3. COMMUNICATE YOUR FEAR OF COMMUNICATING

If you are comfortable, consider talking about your communication phobia. People who know you are also aware of your communication issues. Also, be honest with your anxiety and fear. Acknowledging it right away, before the dialogue begins, will help relieve some of the tension you've built up. The person you talk to will also be more open.

4. THE MORE YOU PRACTICE, THE MORE YOU WILL IMPROVE

Practice, like anything else, makes you better. The more you practice giving difficult speeches, the easier they can become in the long run. Only by consciously focusing on them will you be able to overcome the fear of communication.

5. SEEKING EXTERNAL HELP

Perhaps your fear of communication stems from a deeper problem, such as anxiety or a poor self-image. If you've struggled with the problem your entire life, seeking treatment may be the next step in resolving it. Someone who can handle communication anxiety will provide you with direct, personalized assistance. A life coach or psychologist are excellent figures when it comes to overcoming one's fears.

CHAPTER 6
<u>CHANGE AND IMPROVE YOURSELF</u>

Self-improvement doesn't have to involve drastic changes; it can simply involve taking small steps to improve what you already have in front of you to get you where you want to go. What you will need, however, is perseverance and courage to take on various challenges that will test you.

Rather than setting your long-term goals and getting carried away, you should start taking these practical and effective steps right now.

So, if you want to immediately make a difference in your life and are ready to take action, keep reading, you won't regret it!

- Communication moves you in the right direction. It guides your thoughts and actions.
- You may be influenced by a feeling you've had in the past, such as a painful encounter that triggered a story in your head.
- As a human being with intelligence, it is your responsibility to be careful in the approach you use, both with yourself and with others.
- You have the ability to influence and alter the narrative, just as your thoughts influence who you are and why you are this type of person.
- You can also change the story of your future. Psychologists have found that it is helpful to see yourself in the present and the future as two separate entities when making decisions.

- Changing the way you interact with yourself and others is critical to changing your life and achieving your goals.
- Effective communication skills are important for achieving success in many areas of life. Many professions require excellent communication skills. People who are successful communicators typically have stronger interpersonal relationships with their friends and family.
- Effective communication is therefore a key interpersonal skill, and understanding how to develop communication has many benefits.

Ways to improve yourself that will change your life.

1. Be willing to work hard.

If you want something you have to work hard for it, just like any goal in life. If you want something with your whole self, you have to work hard to get it. What matters here is execution. The more "drive" the action is, the better the results will be in the end.

2. Make sure you have friends to talk to.

As with any self-improvement effort, sharing the load is important. It's great to be able to talk to people and get suggestions on how it's going forward. We also need motivators in our lives to keep us charged up when things get tough, but you still need someone who can tell you the truth even if you don't want to hear it because it's uncomfortable. So, make sure you have a strong support network around you, including those whose opinions you value.

3. Adapt to your circumstances rather than overthinking them.

From time to time we may experience a difficult time. Maybe you lost your job or your girlfriend dumped you. Instead of overthinking the problem, learn to adapt to it and accept it for what it is. It's not about turning the situation into drama; notice that, what you work on spreads, which means you'll get more out of it. You will be much less burdened by your problems if you decide to accept them for what they are.

4. MAKE SURE YOU USE YOUR TIME WISELY.

Some might argue that time is essential, while others argue that time is an illusion. We know you only have one life on this planet, so how you spend that time is important.
Ask yourself how you can make the most of your time.
Only you can do this, but consider how you actually spend your days: do you work all day, come home, eat, and then collapse in front of the TV for the rest of the evening?
Your time on this planet is limited, so isn't it time to make the most of it?
Try something different, like taking a walk, getting in touch with nature, learning a new language or meditating, just make sure it's something you really enjoy and vibe with.

5. ALWAYS BE CONSISTENT.

Improving the way you do things is a great way to improve yourself. For example, with your peers, are you still the unreliable one who backs out of a commitment you've made ? Or are you the type of person who starts a new type of workout and abandons it three weeks later? Be consistent with whatever you do or say. When you make a commitment, stick to it and follow through. It will change your life tremendously; you will feel more confident and satisfied with yourself, especially since you will realize that whatever you tackle you will be able to do it all the way.

6. GO AND FIND YOUR HAPPY PLACE.

No, I don't mean "place," like going to your favorite bar or restaurant and ordering your favorite drinks or foods. What I mean is figuring out what you like to do, what makes you full of life. Your happy place is a place where you can find peace, where you can relax yourself and where you can feel content. Meditation is a great way to find your ideal place; it reconnects you with yourself and ensures that you are still living in the present.

7. BE SURE TO ACCOMMODATE ALL OF YOUR EMOTIONS.

Life will present you with difficult obstacles, sometimes it will drag out your uncertainties and lead you into confusion, and sometimes it will be beautiful. It is important to accept all the feelings in your life, embrace them with all your heart, understand why they are there and then let them go. Try not to ignore them or fight them because, as the saying goes *"What you resist stays."* So, embrace them every time.

8. ALWAYS BE READY TO STEP OUT OF YOUR COMFORT ZONE.

Some people are overwhelmed by the anxiety of stepping out of their comfort zone, but in order to change your life, it's a fundamental step you need to take. It doesn't have to be something huge, like skydiving or something equally crazy. However, it is worth changing something you were afraid of, like going to the movies alone or dining at a sushi restaurant when the idea of trying raw fish usually horrified you.

So do something new, it doesn't have to be grand or adrenaline-pumping, it doesn't have to be an act taken to the limit, it just has to be challenging.

9. BE AVAILABLE TO HELP OTHERS.

Whether it's a stranger on the street, or a family member, or a friend assisting someone else in their time of need, lending a helping hand is a beautiful and easy way to better yourself. Giving to others is beneficial not only to those you are assisting, but also to yourself; it can give you a sense of mission, commitment, and can also keep your mind off your own problems and worries.

10. LIVE IN THE PRESENT.

Living in the present moment, or in the now, is a fantastic self-improvement technique. It is in this moment that you realize what you have and find meaning in the smallest things. Being aware of the present situation and bringing your attention back to where it is, results in a healthier way of living, without anxiety and stress over moments in the past or future, both of which cannot happen. There is only the now, there is only the *Here and Now*. You don't have to live any other way until you have assimilated it and made it your own.

11. LEARN SOMETHING NEW.

There is nothing more liberating than discovering something new, it will boost your morale and self-esteem while still providing a perfect excuse to meet new people. If you constantly stimulate your brain function by learning something different, you can feel on top of your game and want to share what you've learned with others. There's nothing more powerful than discovering a new skill that will increase your circle of friends or boost your confidence, or better yet, both.

12. EXERCISE DAILY.

It may seem intuitive, but exercise is important not only for your well-being but also for your soul. We all know that exercise makes you feel a brighter, more hopeful world, so why don't we do it more often? It's not about having a flawless body or gaining muscle, it's about looking great inside and out. A balanced body leads to a healthy mind, so start today. Whether it's fitness, group classes or just a brisk walk, do it consistently and seriously.

13. GO TO NEW PLACES AND TRAVEL AS MUCH AS YOU CAN.

I'm not suggesting flying to a distant backwater, although you can certainly do that if you wish. It's about seeing new areas and experiencing life outside of your immediate surroundings. Many of us spend too much time in one place. Every day we meet the same people, walk the same streets, and do the same things. Get out and see what the world is doing if you want to change your life. You can start by visiting a city in your nation that you've never seen before, looking at the architecture, the landscapes, and the people. Anything new is good, so explore.

14. LISTEN TO STIMULATING MUSIC AND DANCE.

Listening to inspiring songs and dancing are two things that will really change your life and get you excited. When was the last time you let go completely? That you put everything on hold to lose yourself in a piece of music?

Dancing, like exercise, will cause you to feel good. It arouses a wide range of feelings that can make you feel euphoric. Self-improvement doesn't have to be difficult; it can be as easy as discovering new music that encourages you and makes you want to dance and have fun.

15. GET UP EARLIER THAN USUAL.

This is the last one, and it's one of those self-improvement tips that we all know is healthy, but we tend to ignore at all costs. If you think about it, the first few hours of the day are when your brain is the busiest, since it's been shut down for the previous 7 hours or so. So, don't you think it's wise to get all the most important things handled first thing in the morning? Exercise, yoga, and dance are all activities that should be done in the morning. Trust me: make the morning your time of glory and great productivity.

CHAPTER 7
THE RULES OF ASSERTIVE COMMUNICATION

People give off signals all the time, and learning to recognize those signals is an essential part of the next step we'll be examining.

I have always worked in managerial and executive roles, and this has involved a lot of interaction with other people at various levels, and I never cease to be amazed at how many of them underestimate themselves without even realising it, not being able to communicate successfully.

Many people believe that by being "violent" or "forceful," they can convey their thoughts to another human being and thus support their argument, only to find that it has the opposite effect.

Kindness should be inherent in us at all times of the day.

Sometimes you can accomplish so much more by stepping back and observing how your decisions affect another person. In fact, "seeing and feeling" what you are doing can make a big difference in how you project yourself and live your life, understanding others and how they see you.
You've always heard that most people form an opinion about someone within the first 10 seconds, and the first impression is always the most critical and important one.

So, if that's the case, and people make "instant" decisions, what do others think of me? More specifically, what kind of impact am I having on the people who are important to me?

The good news is that you can do a lot about it, but it is something you will have to work on constantly because depending on how far you want to advance both in your work and in your life in general, the effort you put in will be crucial.

But why do people make these sudden decisions and how do they do it?

According to the classical theory of psychologist Albert Mehrabian it is known that **Non-Verbal** Communication (particularly linked to the body and facial expressions) has an influence of 55% and are messages that are sent unconsciously since they are a large part of our daily routine and our life.

Paraverbal communication on the other hand (tone, volume, rhythm of voice, etc.) is 38% influential which means, people listen to the tone of what you are saying rather than your words. As a result, it's important to be consistent about how you project your voice and body language, as they are all part of the same group. Strong, upbeat body language combined with a powerful voice can often express confidence and authority.

In a conversation, the verbal content, the words you use, count for only 7%.

This is very important news because it means that although you think the words you use are important, they are not important at all and have little effect on what you are saying.

On the other hand, according to Paolo Borzacchiello (author, trainer, leading expert on linguistic intelligence and human interactions, a fine person and a professional whom I hold in great esteem), in his famous book *"Just Say It"*, he completely departs from the classical theory of percentages, defining them as misleading, not to say dangerous.

Again according to Borzacchiello, this is a study that the American psychologist carried out in a specific context and with a specific purpose, namely to see how significant, when talking about emotions, was the facial expression of the person talking about them. In this regard, Mehrabian himself specified that those percentages, in other contexts, had no value. And he even had to write publicly that he was *"disheartened by the use of his percentages by self-styled experts"*.

Having clarified this, let us continue with our book.

Before communicating anything, it is important to understand what our goals and priorities are.

Being an assertive person is part of the Win-Win dynamic in which two people decide to find an agreement and a compromise between two opposing needs that can satisfy both.

It is worth remembering that effective assertive communication requires attention to five rules:

1. We listen to people in an interested mode because it is the only way to understand their point of view. For this purpose, we can use some typical coaching strategies such as rephrasing (*If I understood you correctly you are telling me that...*); formulating questions on unclear aspects (*If I*

understood you correctly you want me to...); summarising at the end of the conversation to emphasise the most important concepts and give feedback.

2. We always speak in the first person using phrases such as *"I would like this work to be completed within the week"*. When we have a different opinion we replace *"You are wrong"* with *"I disagree"* to make it clear that we are not judging.

3. We express our needs clearly and concretely in order to make it easier for others to understand and create the conditions to avoid misunderstandings.

4. We communicate our No in a direct manner and always accompany it with a clear reason. We could then say: *'I cannot stay later than 6 p.m. because I have already made a commitment'.*
5. Let's pay attention to the words we use and non-verbal language. As Borzacchiello states: *"The words you use say where you come from, the words you choose say where you want to go"*. With regard to body language, maintaining eye contact, an open posture, facial expressions, and a firm, assertive tone of voice come in handy.

Knowing how to communicate assertively is an art that everyone can learn.

CHAPTER 8
LISTEN CAREFULLY

"If a fool holds his tongue, he will pass for wise."
Publilius Syrus Roman Emperor.

Most people are aware of the value of being assertive in social situations. Having one's needs addressed in a caring and constructive manner is one of the first topics that comes to mind when people talk about "being assertive". It can be challenging to take an assertive approach in interpersonal relationships for people who struggle to see themselves as bossy. It is important to note that assertiveness requires a careful combination of asserting one's own interests and being aware of the needs of others.

Perhaps the other person's desires, urgent interests will take precedence over the ability to explicitly state their needs first. When you think the person you are conversing with is overwhelmed by their own desires, this is an opportunity to practice assertive listening. When you take part in this form of active listening, you briefly set aside your own desires, thoughts, and statuses to fully absorb the other person's perspective. This way your desires will usually be more easily met in the end. Before being able to fulfill requests, people want to feel that they have been respected and that their point of view has been acknowledged.

ASSERTIVE LISTENING

When practicing assertive listening, focus your attention on your interlocutor so that you can properly listen to his or her thoughts, ideas, and desires.

It uses the following three steps for this purpose:

1. PREPARE

Prepare yourself physically, intellectually, and socially to listen to what the other person has to say. Make sure you are not overwhelmed by your own desires as you consciously focus all your attention on the other person.

When you are certain you are ready to listen, make sure they are ready to share their insights. Don't assume that your speaker is able to communicate with you at any given time just because you are. Paying attention to your own (the listener's) and the other person's (the speaker's) interests in a thoughtful and conscious way is part of assertive listening. Check in with in a friendly way, *"Maybe you have something on your mind that you'd like to talk about. Please let me know if you have something to say. "*

2. LISTEN AND CLARIFY

When you listen assertively and deliberately, you are tuning into the present. Give the other person your undivided attention by listening carefully to their thoughts, desires, and points of view. Put your own opinion aside for a moment to really empathize with the other party. Allow yourself to briefly defer judgment on the "validity" of their complaints and listen.

If you have doubts about what they are saying, ask questions. People usually like it when others ask about their experiences, particularly when those requests stem from a sincere desire to understand. If you're confused, you might ask them to explain themselves again with something as simple as *"I'm not sure I understand your point of view. Could you please explain?"*

3. RECOGNIZE

When you are certain that you have heard the other person's point of view, thoughts, and feelings, say so. Actively communicate to the other party that you have considered and understood their thoughts. Continue to not express your decisions and avoid getting too stuck in your role. Validate their experience without interfering or attempting to "correct" anything.

For some people, seeing their experience reconfirmed in this way can be a very powerful relief. Some people struggle with intense impulses to "fix" problems, especially when they affect the people they care for. Resist this urge by understanding that sometimes the surest way to show empathy and support to others is to actually listen to what they have to say and state their point of view.

Every moment is an incentive to learn a new way to communicate with others.

Take note the next time you find yourself in a situation where:

- The other seems to have something important to say.
- You are forced to interrupt or express your point of view.
- You are concerned about your feelings, emotions, and desires.
- You feel detached from the other person and like you don't fully understand them.

Take a step back from the situation and assess whether you and the other party are able to communicate. Listen to your interlocutor actively and then assertively, check with them for any misunderstandings. When you believe you have really listened and understood what he has to say, reflect on his perspective and let him know you meant it.

Listening is one of the most valuable qualities you can have as you perceive what people are really thinking and saying. The way you listen has a significant influence on your business success and the nature of your relationships with others.

For example:

- We listen for information.
- We listen to understand.
- We listen for fun.
- We listen to learn.

In reality, most of us are flawed in this ability, and according to leading researchers we only remember between 25% and

50% of what we listen to. This means that if you talk to your manager at work, your family, your clients or your partner for 10 minutes, they only listen to half of what you're saying.

Turn the tables and you'll see that when you're given instructions or details, you're not listening to the entire message.

Clearly, listening is a trait that we all could stand to improve. You must increase your effectiveness and your ability to control, persuade and negotiate by becoming a skilled and attentive listener. You must also avoid confrontations and misunderstandings. All of these skills are necessary for success in your professional, as well as personal, life.

You can't allow yourself to be disturbed by what is happening around you or to counter-argue while your speaker is speaking. You also cannot allow yourself to get bored and lose focus on what the speaker is doing.

Tip: If you have trouble focusing on what someone is doing, start mentally repeating their phrases as they say them. This will continue to validate their message and keep you engaged by communicating to the other person that you are paying attention to what they are doing.

Recognition can be as simple as a nod of the head or a simple 'yes-yes'. Using body language and other signs that you are listening will also help you pay attention.
Act with the speaker in a way that encourages him/her to continue communicating so that you can get the answers

you need. If your nods and "yeses" show that you are interested, an occasional question or statement to summarise what he said makes it clear that you are listening and understanding his message.

BECOME AN ACTIVE LISTENER

Active listening is when you listen beyond the words being spoken to understand the meaning being conveyed. During interviews, 'the listener' is often preoccupied with how to react rather than focusing on what the speaker is saying.

By really listening, you get a more insightful response that takes into account the speaker's opinions and thoughts.

There are five main active listening strategies you can use to become a better listener:

1. PAY ATTENTION

- Give your full attention to the speaker and accept the message.
- Recognize that nonverbal speech also "speaks" aloud.
- Look directly at who is speaking.
- Set aside distracting emotions.
- Avoid being disturbed by environmental factors and secondary conversations.
- Pay attention to the speaker's body language.

2. SHOW THAT YOU'RE LISTENING

- Use body language and gestures to show you care.
- Nod from time to time.
- Give a smile.
- Make sure your posture is open and engaged.

- Encourage the speaker to continue with small verbal comments such as "yes-yes" and "uh-huh."

3. PROVIDE FEEDBACK

What we hear will be distorted by our filters, assumptions, judgments, experiences and values. Your job as a listener is to understand what is being said and what it is trying to transfer. This should require you to reflect on what is being reported and ask questions.

- Effective means of reflection can be *"What I'm thinking is ..." and "You seem to be thinking ..."*
- To resolve your doubts, ask questions like *"What do you mean by that?"*
- Periodically summarize the speaker's comments.

Tip:

If you find yourself reacting negatively to what someone does, speak up. Also, request more information such as, *"I may have misunderstood you"*, *"I took what you said personally"*, *"What I misunderstood was..." or "What did you mean?"*

4. DEFERRING JUDGMENT

Interrupting is something that should never be done. It irritates the speaker and prevents the complete understanding of the message.

- Before answering questions, let the speaker finish each step.
- Interruption of counter-arguments is not permitted.

5. RESPOND APPROPRIATELY

Active listening is meant to foster empathy and understanding. You are gaining knowledge and perspective. By insulting or otherwise denigrating the speaker you are not contributing anything positive at all.

- In your response, be frank, transparent and honest.
- Respectfully express your thoughts.
- Treat the other party the way you think they would want to be treated.

CHAPTER 9
SPEAK IN THE FIRST PERSON

One of the fundamental and useful points in assertive communication is first person. I'm referring to when a person uses the pronouns: I, me, we, and our, to speak explicitly to their interlocutor and tell their story or update themselves on what is happening.

"I" PHRASES

People will irritate you, disappoint you, and disrespect you. They may do it unintentionally but they will do it anyway. In these moments, you have the option to remain silent and allow the anger to get worse (the best way to deteriorate a relationship and frustrate you), or you can choose to speak up. The problem with speaking up is that even if you have the right intentions, communicating reactively and ineffectively will exacerbate the misunderstanding, hurt the people you care about, and gradually diminish the strength of your relationships.

Using a request through "I-phrases" is a perfect tactic for accepting responsibility in relationships and asking for your wishes to be met (even as a request for a change in behavior).

Specifically in the parent-child relationship, the calmer a parent communicates with their child, the better it is for the child to hear, understand and assimilate the message. We want our children to interact and cooperate with us and that makes them happy. People of all ages enjoy the shared love and gratitude that comes from cooperation and teamwork, especially when they feel appreciated for their contributions.

When we share our feelings about children's requests, limits, and suggestions, it can be very helpful to use "I-phrases" as it is a non-blaming, non-critical, and shameless way to express our thoughts and perspectives.

Limits and requests conveyed with genuine concern for the child make them feel more invited and active, rather than manipulated and coerced. If they need additional information or assistance before working with us, the child may feel more free to ask and get what they need to do what is required.

Although calm communication works best, parents can sometimes be irritated or angry with their child. This is normal as they may experience moments of fatigue, depression, and a sense of emptiness with less clarity and more need for support. It is natural for this to happen when parents feel overwhelmed trying to meet the needs of their entire family. As long as parents maintain their general position as mature and loving adults, which involves rebuilding the bond and resolving misunderstandings after confrontation, our children can not only cope with us by providing emotional reactions to family problems, but they can also learn a lot from these experiences.

WHAT "I-PHRASES" COMMUNICATE TO OTHERS

By using "I-phrases" you take responsibility for how you act and think. These statements allow you to consider your desires and expectations, clarify the situation with confidence, and present an action-oriented perspective. Listening as a recipient to "I-phrases" sheds light on how your own behaviors have influenced the speaker.

"I-phrases" offer the receiver insight into the speaker's emotions and experiences, encourages the listener to empathize with the communicator, and opens the door to conversation.

In general, it is up to you to present an assertive and polite submission, and it is up to your partner/colleague to respond naturally. While there is no guarantee that your interlocutor will always respond productively and fulfill your requests, following the next script will maximize the likelihood of having a fruitful dialogue that will yield great benefits.

ADVANTAGES OF USING "I-PHRASES"

"I-phrases" are a means of expressing to your child in a simple, genuine and assertive but non-aggressive way your requests, boundaries and limitations. The parent expresses their emotions and serves as the perfect role model on how to convey feelings without attacking, demanding, insulting, or punishing. An example of a "first-person" statement is, *"When you talk to me like this, I feel sad/frustrated,"* as opposed to a "second-person" statement, such as, *"You are too rude, don't talk to me like that."* Alternatively, you can say, *"I'm annoyed because we decided you were going to turn the music down when I was on the phone, but you turned it up and I couldn't hear anything,"* as opposed to *"How can I trust you when we had an agreement? It was absolutely rude of you to turn the music up like that."*

"I-phrases" are less likely to elicit a protective response from both the child and the adult.

- Because it feels less blamed.
- Because the interaction is more mature and elevated, without harsh signals or statements.
- Because it allows the child to see the adult for who they are.
- Because it encourages more open communication than "you-phrases."

American clinical psychologist Thomas Gordon established useful instructions for expressing "first person" sentences:

- Assure your child that you trust and care about them (if applicable).
- Express what you see or the actual event that happened.
- Express how you feel about what you see or what has happened.
- Express why you feel the way you do.
- Give your child the ability to improve their behavior or engage in conversation because of this information.
- Tell your child what you want from him, but only if he fails on his own.

SOME PRACTICAL EXAMPLES ARE:

- *"Because your play is so loud* (information), *I'm worried* (your feeling) *that the child will wake up and be nervous* (reason for emotion), *although it's nice that you're having fun* (reassurance to take care of his wishes)."

- *"When I see you running in* (information), *I worry* (how you feel) *that you might break something or fall and hurt yourself* (ensuring care)*".*
- *"I see you're having fun with your games, and now that it's 6:30, I'd like you to finish your homework. Do you want to go over it with me?"*
- *"I heard that you want me to play with you. I'm sorry* (your feeling) *because I would love to* (reassurance that you want a connection), *but I need to make dinner and I can't do both."*
- *"It makes me sad when I give you food and you say 'yuck'...".* If there is no response, continue. *"How else can you tell me you don't like carrots?"*
- *"I worry when I see you putting crayons in your mouth; they're just for drawing and can make you sick."* If there is no answer, continue. *"You should draw with crayons but not in your mouth."*

THE FIVE CRITICAL PHASES FORMULA

1. *"While you..."*- Describes the exact behavior taken by your partner.

2. *"I feel..."* - Shares how you inwardly feel in reaction to the action. It is important to remember that feelings are NOT decisions and can be expressed separately. Sadness, sorrow, joy, satisfaction, anger, fear and other emotions are examples. Judgments are the lies you tell yourself about what the other person's actions mean to you and the relationship. Your emotions are driven by the stories you tell yourself.
If you pay attention to the way people talk, you will find that we often confuse feelings with assumptions through our use of "I feel" phrases.

3. *"What I am telling myself is...."* - Accept responsibility for your decisions about other people and circumstances by sharing and examining them. This involves admitting that although you may feel a certain way, you may still misinterpret the situation and have an incorrect judgment about the other person's actions (we rarely have all the information at any given time). When you frankly state what you believe is happening for you, you encourage your partner to consider your point of view and address any misunderstandings.

4. *"I need to... please"*- Expresses what you want from the context. Before sending a message, it is your duty to determine what you need and want. It is not your interlocutor's duty to decipher your mind and identify your desires and emotions (especially if you are holding back or pretending that things are going well when they are not). Few

people are better than others at picking up on what isn't being said, and the circumstances of everyday life can also make this very difficult. Don't mistake someone's inability to read your mind for a lack of consideration for you. Learn to understand people's reactions to your requests, that is, dwell on their actions rather than their words.

If your counterpart has improved his behaviour, it means that he has listened to you and has made an effort over time to strengthen his dialogue and interaction with you.

5. *"Can you... "* - Choose a clear action for your partner to perform. Make sure the proposal is fair and has a deadline, which involves checking in with your partner to see if it is feasible. A request can be difficult to complete depending on what's going on in the other person's life. For this reason, try to be versatile about how your needs are being met.

Keep your questions short, clear, and relevant.

FEWER "YOU-PHRASES" LEAD TO LESS STRESS

Without learning a different or better way to communicate, parents to children, but sometimes even between adults, can depend too much on "you-phrases" like *"you have to ...", "you shouldn't ...", "why should you still . .", "because ...", "now you need.... ", "you make me angry when.... ", "you make me nervous when ...", "you better fix it now", "you need to do your homework", "you need to make your bed", "this is not how you should do it".*

Too many "you-phrases" can sound critical and accusatory and can be very discouraging. So many 'you-sentences' make it impossible for anyone to grasp your emotions, understand your interests and evaluate your point of view.

Giving your child too many orders, demands, and corrections puts you as a parent in the position of staff sergeant, making it difficult, if not impossible, for your child to maintain a sense of your humanity. One of the challenges of parenting is being a solid, trusting, compassionate, and fair leader while maintaining trust, free contact, and attachment.

Using such "you-phrases" usually mean that you are blaming the person you are referring to for how you feel. These comments seem to center the discussion on guilt, criticism, and a defensive attitude. When someone says, *"You're not listening to me,"* your gut reaction is to say, *"Of course I'm listening."*

When you are upset or hurt, "you-phrases" may seem normal as a go to comeback but when you use these statements, you stop being open by not taking responsibility for acknowledging and truly expressing your needs. "You-phrases" attempt to make the receiver justify their own conduct and character. It also makes it more difficult for the receiver to listen and respond to the speaker's basic needs.

CHAPTER 10
EXPRESS YOUR NEEDS CLEARLY AND CONCISELY

Have you ever been quiet so you could keep your cool? Have you ever felt like your point of view didn't matter? Have you "let it go" to avoid an argument?
This can occur at home, with friends and family, at work, or in all cases.

How can you go from biting your tongue to opening up a conversation and showing people how you really feel?

Conflict is always difficult to deal with and we can try at all costs to prevent it. Our upbringing and background can influence our responses, behavior, willingness and ability to stay close to one another until a peaceful discussion is reached.

It is possible that you have learned to avoid confrontation and awkward circumstances. Maybe you come from a family where disagreements were resolved in violent ways. Maybe you felt terrified as a child and didn't know what to do. Unfortunately, there are few opportunities in our society and culture to teach children emotional literacy, forcing them to learn it on their own to the best of their ability. As adults, this can lead to latent inner worries and limiting expectations.

PERCEPTION IS EVERYTHING

Our perceptions are as individual as our lives. Everything that happens inside and outside of us is perceived differently by everyone. As a result, there is a generalization because when it comes to thoughts, emotions, and meeting our needs, things may not be so simple.

Even if we use the same language, we can't use the same words we use to describe ourselves. Even if we don't want to be hurtful, violent, aggressive, or overbearing, our words may have that effect on others.

American psychologist, Marshall B. Rosenburg, established a precise method of communication and listening that he called Non-violent Communication. This method encourages us to communicate with our hearts, binds us to each other and to ourselves in such a way that natural compassion develops.

Nonviolent Communication (NCV) helps you be present in the situation rather than acting on habitual unconscious responses.

When we are self-aware, we are more aware of how we feel and what feelings we have. We are much more likely to realize our needs and be able to express them in a way that can be understood by everyone. In essence, through this method, we will be able to listen and empathize with the thoughts and desires of others.

The Four components of the CNV are:

- *Observation:* Observe what is happening in a situation without making judgments or evaluations.
- *Feeling:* Express how you feel when you experience a situation, such as whether you are hurt, depressed, or happy.
- *Needs:* Communicate your needs and values in relation to the situation.
- *Request:* Make a special proposal to meet the requirements.

When we apply this concept to ourselves and ask others to do the same, we will increase our levels of connectivity and empathy.

Non-violent dialogue is applicable in all contexts, from families and friends to colleagues. The four components include a framework that allows us to articulate ourselves simply, efficiently and effectively, while also cultivating empathy, sensitivity and interaction, all essential skills in today's world.

THERE IS ALWAYS A DIFFERENT WAY OF LOOKING AT THINGS

Self-limiting beliefs are only that way because you make them that way, it's your responsibility. Have you ever felt frustrated and uncomfortable when you tried to bring about changes at work, or just when you introduced or implemented new ways of communicating?

Introducing an alternative way of doing things in the workplace can be difficult. We often slip into self-limiting habits (of action, thought, and relationships) because we have legacies about what we can and cannot do. We get caught up in assumptions surrounding these beliefs, especially in what people would think of us if we acted differently than the standard.

Do you have self-limiting beliefs or perceptions about the work culture and/or aspirations of those you work for? Commit to understanding your thoughts about these views. It's possible that these beliefs are hindering your desire to model a new way of doing things.

Recognize your self-limiting assumptions about how work should be done in your office. As these beliefs emerge, consider how they might affect your ability to model a more rewarding way of talking to your colleagues. Be empathetic and ask yourself to test whether that belief is valid and has reason to exist.

CHAPTER 11
COMMUNICATE YOUR "NO" EFFECTIVELY

Being helpful to others and providing practical help is a good thing, but it can often lead to irritating moods. So much so that studies have shown that frequently providing assistance to other people makes you feel taken advantage of. Even when you're only getting a colleague's attention, you can feel under emotional strain, especially when you're the subject of "toxic treatment," (a phrase invented by psychologists to characterize the people everyone complains about).

Either way, if you're in it, it can be hard to get out of it. Telling people no, after you've told them yes for your time and attention, can be a problem.

Trying to please everyone, on the other hand, is just as unhealthy as eating fast food all the time. Pleasing others (or even trying to please everyone) often leaves you feeling disappointed and vulnerable.

Maybe you're wondering how you can say no and not feel bad? To answer this question, you need to consider that people believe it is wrong to say no. Saying no, as if you're denying the person, can feel hurtful, as if you're letting someone down in fear of not being considered or appreciated. As a result, people almost always try to agree as much as possible.

If people say no, they normally do so through an ineffective excuse. They might say, *"I'd like to help but I'm too busy."* The flaw in this solution is that it allows the other person to inquire. There is an opportunity, they think. *"Since you're busy this week, how about next week?"*

THE ADVANTAGES OF SAYING NO

You are perfectly aware that you have to take care of yourself and your work before you can devote your resources to helping others. You should say no more often.
However, if you do, the other person may feel hurt. He or she may change their mind about you. You may even lose the sense of connection in the relationship. Right?

According to Vanessa Bohns, associate professor at Cornell University, that's not the case. *"People don't take no as badly as we think they do," she said. "It's likely that the consequences of saying 'no' in our minds are even worse than they are in reality."* Think about it.

So, if you're going to be programming on the computer instead of hanging out with your coworkers, just say no. They won't mind at all. If you have an important task to tackle, say no to lazy peers who dump their duties on others. Eventually they'll find another scapegoat.

HERE ARE FOUR MORE GOOD REASONS TO SAY NO:

1. Maintain control.
YOU, not your friends or colleagues, know what is best for you. Saying no to what you don't want allows you to focus on what you really like. As a result, you maintain control over your life rather than allowing others to do so.

2. You are happy.

Rejecting the things you don't want to do frees up time for the things you prefer. The Dalai Lama believes that having more of what you like and less of what you don't like will make you more comfortable. And it's satisfaction that contributes to prosperity, rather than being the other way around.

3. Get Respect.

To make your "yes" meaningful, you need to say "no" more often.

People will appreciate you once they know you're not an easy yes man. And they will choose the activities for which they seek your help.

4. Hello, hello, negative people.

Saying no has a two-fold impact. For starters, it allows you to focus on what you really want.

Second, it helps identify those who deserve to be in your life. Don't feel sorry for yourself if you refuse their requests. However, all those who are offended are free to leave.

SAYING NO WITHOUT FEELING GUILTY

Now that we've identified the benefits, let's elaborate on how to say no assertively.

1. REJECT THE REQUEST, NOT THE PERSON.

Make it clear in your mind and in the words you use that you are rejecting the proposal, not the person. Look the person in the eye, smile spontaneously, and make it clear why you are rejecting the request. Acknowledge that the shame you feel is entirely of your own making.

To soften the blow that comes from rejection, start with a *"I wish I could, but..."*

2. BE IMPASSIVE ONCE YOU MAKE A DECISION.

Don't change your mind and be consistent. Being strong in a kind way is part of successfully saying no. There is no vanity here, only firmness. If you are persuaded against your will, someone will see a weakness and use it against you. And you'll end up right back where you started.
If you said yes, stay in the present and bring your duty to fruition. You have no other options, so you may as well give it your all.

3. OFFER AN ALTERNATIVE.

You don't like the restaurant where your friends want to eat. In these cases, present alternatives. For example, *"I don't like the restaurant because the service is poor. Why don't we go to that other one?"* Another example: If a colleague asks for assistance when you're short on time, tell them, *"I'm on a deadline unfortunately. If no one else can help you, come back on Thursday. We'll work on it more carefully."*

Can you see what I mean? Isn't it easier that way?

4. DELAYED RESPONSE.

We human beings are impulsive creatures by nature. We always act hastily, only to regret our actions later. A hasty "yes" could drown you in a flood of work. An instant "no" might cause you to rethink your decision.

Take your time in making a call. Evaluate the advantages and disadvantages. According to science, sleeping on it is a great way to do it.

5. PRACTICE ON YOURSELF FIRST.

To say no to others, you must first say no to yourself. Avoid wasting money on things you don't need. Say no to whipped cream in your coffee when you need to stick to a low-calorie diet. When you can walk, don't take a cab.
According to studies, the greater your willpower, the easier it is to say no. So work on strengthening your willpower.

The key to saying no without hurting others is to relax.

Practice in front of the mirror. Listen to yourself. Observe your nonverbal communication. Does your body stiffen? Does your mouth twitch? Do you pout? These are signs of tension.
Regular practice will help you relax your body and mind.

Above all, ask yourself what is important to you: your own fulfillment or pleasing everyone?

No one likes everyone. Even Michael Jackson, Barack Obama and Nelson Mandela had their vilifiers. You're no different from them. So stop trying.

Instead, make time to do what makes you happy. Prioritize your work to move forward in both your personal and professional life. Choose between what is important and what is not. Say yes to one and no to the other, according to your will. Believe me when I say saying no is not as hard as it seems.

Don't spend the rest of your time trying to fulfill the desires of others. It's time for you to start fulfilling your own.

CHAPTER 12
<u>NON-VERBAL LANGUAGE</u>

Assertiveness is described as the ability to assert oneself through persuasion, directing choices, and gaining the consent of others without being abusive or violent. An individual who is not assertive can often be one of two things: aggressive or passive. In today's society, slipping into either of these extremes is detrimental and would often prevent you from getting the things you desire in life.
A passive individual is someone most people can ignore. People will often harass you if they believe you are vulnerable or easy to manipulate. Passive individuals are more likely to have low self-esteem.

Aggressive individuals are the other side of the coin. Although these people are quick to protect themselves and their interests, they often do so in a way that offends a large number of people.

Although aggressive people are always more successful than passive people, ofyen times their triumph is not complete. They attract so many enemies in the process that their victory becomes fleeting. Another problem with violent individuals is that they often claim that their own opinions and emotions are more important than those of others.

Nonverbal assertive communication is a communication style in which you assert yourself without saying anything. This type of assertiveness requires the use of body language to effectively convey your message.

Nonverbal communication includes gestures, facial expressions, tone of voice, eye contact (or lack thereof), body language, posture, and other methods of nonverbal communication.

Nonverbal contact is just as crucial as verbal communication when applying for a job, attending a conference, or even in the day-to-day business environment.

In fact, your non-verbal communication skills have the potential to have a constructive or negative impact. Crossed arms may appear to be a method of defence. Bad posture will give the impression that you are unprofessional. Focusing downwards or avoiding eye contact will distract from your perception of confidence.

If your skills are not up to the mark, you should improve them so that you have a good impact on everyone you meet. Establishing reputation and trust is a critical success factor in many professions. Non-verbal signals (such as eye contact) will help you convey your honesty and engaging personality.

Do you need skill training? Go through this list of non-verbal skills and focus on any items you feel you can develop:

- Avoid leaning back. To express commitment, sit with your back straight against the chair or gently lean forward.
- Avoid smiles or laughter when messages are serious.
- Project a serious and professional appearance by showing some hand movements and facial expressions. (However, stop communicating with your hands unnecessarily and in excess, as this will make you look unprofessional and unpolished).

- Don't bring your phone or anything else that might distract you during an interview or conference.
- Eliminates fidgeting and shaking of limbs.
- Maintain regular but not constant or penetrating eye contact with interviewers.
- Focus on the conversation.
- In a group interview, move eye contact to the various speakers.
- Greet everyone with a smile and a handshake.
- Keep your hands away from your face and hair.
- Listen carefully and don't interrupt.
- Keep your arms open: folded arms can convey a defensive attitude.
- Change the sound of your voice to convey enthusiasm and to emphasize important points.
- Give a nod to show understanding.

It is also important to observe the reaction of others to your statements:

- Recognize others' nonverbal cues. If they are puzzled, provide an explanation and see if they have understood enough.
- Refrain from forced laughter in response to humor.
- Don't look at the time, your phone, or show other symptoms of boredom.
- Be aware of how much personal space your stakeholders want.
- In group interviews, shift eye contact between the different speakers.
- Wave your hands vigorously to give strength to some passages but not violently.
- Demonstrates interest in what the interviewer is saying.

- Use a smile to show that you are amused or delighted by the interaction. Keep your cool even when you're nervous.
- Avoid monotonous answers.
- Wait until the person has finished speaking to respond.

COMMUNICATING AT JOB INTERVIEWS

During a job interview, your nonverbal messages will either reinforce the sound of your conversation or leave the interviewer wondering if you're just "all talk and no action." Nonverbal actions that complement your messages will help persuade managers, showing that you're truly invested in the job and qualified for that position.

Another recruitment consideration is the obvious desire of the candidate to communicate easily with employers and colleagues.

Subtly mirroring the body language of interviewers, for example, will make you seem more trustworthy to them. Similarly, a lack of eye contact indicates a lack of interest and an inability to fully communicate with others.

In general, the most important thing is to be upbeat and engaging. If you're confident in your ability to do the job well and believe you can be an asset and value-add to the company, you'll prove it through your actions and speech.

Practice makes perfect, and doing this with counselors, friends, and colleagues will help you hone your nonverbal communication skills. Try to monitor practice sessions so you can analyze any changes in style.

Spending time on training means that your skills are up to date. You will probably be more comfortable during interviews or at plenary meetings if you have spent time preparing. The less stressed you are, the better your communication skills will be, both verbal and non-verbal.

TIPS FOR IMPROVING NONVERBAL COMMUNICATION

Strong listening skills can benefit you in both your personal and professional life. Although verbal and written communication skills are critical, studies have found that nonverbal activities are a significant part of our daily interpersonal communication.

In order to develop your nonverbal communication skills the following tips will help you learn how to decipher the nonverbal signals of others and improve your ability to communicate effectively.

PAY ATTENTION TO NON-VERBAL CUES

People can convey information in a variety of ways, so pay attention to eye contact, gestures, posture, body expressions, and tone of voice. All of these signals convey vital information that cannot be expressed in words.

You will increase your ability to interact if you pay more attention to nonverbal habits.

SEARCH FOR INCONSISTENT BEHAVIOR

When words struggle to follow nonverbal cues, people seem to ignore what has been said in favor of unspoken representations of moods, feelings, and emotions. When someone says one thing but their body posture shows another, it can be helpful to pay close attention to such implicit nonverbal signals. For example, someone may tell you they are happy while frowning and looking at the floor.

FOCUS ON YOUR TONE OF VOICE

Your tone of voice can express a myriad of information, ranging from excitement to disinterest to anger. Tone can be a powerful tool to amplify your message.

Start noticing how your tone of voice affects how people react and try using your voice to emphasize the thoughts you want to share.

For example, if you want to show a genuine interest in something, use an animated tone of voice. These signals can express your feelings about a topic, but they can, even more so, stimulate the interest of your listener.

USE GOOD EYE CONTACT

Another important nonverbal communication skill is maintaining good eye contact. When individuals struggle to look someone in the eye, it can feel like they are avoiding or hiding something. Too much eye contact, on the other hand, can seem confrontational or threatening.

Although eye contact is a vital aspect of conversation, keep in mind that successful eye contact does not involve staring into someone's eyes. So how do you figure out how much eye contact to make?

Some communication specialists prescribe eye contact periods of four or five seconds. Effective visual communication should come across as normal and relaxed with both you and the person you are communicating with.

ASK QUESTIONS

If you are puzzled by nonverbal signals to the other person, don't be afraid to ask. It's smart to reiterate your understanding of what was said and ask clearly. Here are some examples:

- *"So, you're saying..."*
- *"You mean we should..."*
- *"So you think..."*

Simply asking such questions can also provide a wealth of information about a situation.

For example, a person might send nonverbal signals when they are thinking about something else. You may have a better idea of what they are trying to explain if you delve deeper into their message and purpose.

USE SIGNALS TO ADD MEANING

Keep in mind that both verbal and nonverbal speech are used to communicate the message. Body language that emphasizes and encourages what you are doing will help you strengthen your verbal communication. This is especially helpful when giving speeches or presenting in front of a large number of people.

For example, if you want to appear calm and prepared during a presentation, you should focus on conveying nonverbal cues that will assure people who see you a feeling of confidence and professionalism. You should project feelings of confidence by doing the following:

- Staying fixed in one position.
- Keep your shoulders back.
- Keep the weight balanced on both feet.

LOOK AT THE SIGNALS AS A WHOLE

Another critical aspect of nonverbal communication, is the ability to look at what someone is doing from a broader perspective. A single gesture can mean a variety of things or none at all.

Looking for groups of signals that confirm a particular argument is a secret to correctly interpreting nonverbal behavior. If you focus so much on one or more signals, you can come to the wrong conclusion about what someone is trying to communicate.

CONSIDER THE CONTEXT

When dealing with others, try to understand the situation and the context in which the conversation takes place. Some cases call for more rigid behaviors, which may be understood very differently in another context.

Think about what nonverbal actions are appropriate for the situation. If you want to strengthen your nonverbal communication, focus on adapting your signals to the degree of formality required by the situation.

Body language and nonverbal contact, for example, are certainly somewhat different from the gestures you would make on a casual Friday night with friends. Strive to tailor your nonverbal signals to the situation to ensure you're conveying the message you really want to convey.

BE AWARE THAT SIGNALS CAN BE MISUNDERSTOOD

Some believe that a firm handshake shows a confident personality, while a poor handshake indicates a lack of fortitude. This example emphasizes a crucial topic regarding the likelihood of misinterpreting nonverbal signals. A shaky handshake may be an indication of something else, such as arthritis.

Always keep an eye on behavioral clusters. An individual's overall attitude is much more revealing than a single action viewed in isolation.

Nonverbal communication skills are important for conveying your point of view and understanding what others are trying to tell you. Some people seem to be born with these skills, but everyone can develop their nonverbal skills with practice.

CHAPTER 13
<u>VERBAL LANGUAGE</u>

Verbal communication is the use of language to exchange ideas with others. Consequently, it should involve both oral and written components. However, many people use speech to refer only to verbal conversation. The verbal component of communication is about the words you chose and how they are understood and translated.

Verbal communication is a form of oral communication in which meaning is conveyed by spoken words. The sender communicates his or her emotions, impressions, concepts, and points of view through speeches, debates, interviews, and conversations.

The effectiveness of verbal communication is determined by the speaker's accent, understanding of voice, pace, timing, body language, and consistency of the words used in the dialogue. In the case of the verbal component, feedback is instantaneous as the sender and receiver simultaneously transmit and receive the message.

This section addresses the verbal component. However, for the written component, where there is little or no verbal communication to aid in understanding the message, the use of words may be helpful, if not more essential.

The sender must keep his or her voice style high and clearly understood by all, and the topic must be designed with the target audience in mind. The sender can always double-check with the recipient to make sure the message was understood exactly as intended. Such communication is more susceptible to errors because the words themselves do not always convey a person's thoughts and emotions.

Success in verbal communication depends not only on an individual's ability to speak, but also on their listening skills. The effectiveness of speech is determined by how well a person listens to the topic.
The better your listening skills, the greater the likelihood of success in the workplace both at the interview stage and in career advancement.
In business contexts, Human Resources (HR) managers place a high priority on employees and managers who can communicate facts accurately and efficiently; in fact it is an essential soft skill for any advanced company.

To summarize, we can say that verbal communication refers to any mode of communication in which words are used to exchange information with others. These words can be expressed or printed.
Effective verbal communication requires more than just words. Verbal contact includes how signals are sent and how they are received.
Those who can read messages and respond correctly to the information they receive are more likely to succeed in all areas of life.

Verbal communication is important as we use it to educate others about our desires or to convey information. Clarification is an essential part of verbal communication.
We can't always express ourselves effectively, or our comments or actions are misunderstood. Verbal

communication helps clear up misunderstandings and provide lost information.

Verbal communication should be used to correct a mistake, where strong phrases are more successful than action. It can also be used as a persuasive weapon, stimulating dialogue, prompting reflection and imagination, and deepening and establishing new relationships.

VERBAL COMMUNICATION SKILLS IN THE WORKPLACE

What constitutes successful verbal contact at work is determined by relationships with coworkers and the context of the job.

In the workplace, verbal contact occurs among a variety of people and organizations, including colleagues, supervisors and subordinates, staff, consumers, employers, teachers and students, speakers, and their audiences.

Verbal communication occurs in a variety of ways, including educational seminars, workshops, group meetings, performance evaluations, individual consultations, interviews, disciplinary hearings, sales appeals, and counseling appointments.

Here are some examples of positive organizational verbal communication skills in various work settings.

Verbal Communications for Supervisors: The greatest leaders never tell their subordinates what to do or ask them to do it. Instead, they use constructive communication skills to consider staff expectations and viewpoints, participate in verbal negotiation to resolve and defuse problems, and use opportunities to recognize individual and team accomplishments.

In particular:

- Advise others regarding an appropriate course of action.
- Be assertive.
- Constructively convey feedback by emphasizing specific and changing behaviors.
- Discipline employees in a direct and respectful manner.
- Give credit to others.
- Recognize and counter objections.
- Show interest in others, investigate and acknowledge their emotions.
- Speak calmly even when stressed.
- Train others to perform a task or role.
- Use affirmative sounds and words such as "uh-huh," "I hear you," "I understand," "sure," and "yes" to show understanding.
- Use self-revelation to encourage sharing.

Verbal Communications for Team Members: Open and consistent lines of communication are critical to team progress, particularly when completing quality and deadline-sensitive tasks. Effective interpersonal contact is one of the most valuable team-building skills because it helps ensure that problems are identified and addressed in the early stages, avoiding worrisome escalations.

In particular:

- Convey messages in a concise manner.
- Encourage reluctant group members to help with their contributions.
- Explain a difficult situation without getting angry.
- Explain that you need assistance.
- Paraphrase to show understanding.
- Ask probing questions to get more detail on specific issues.
- Receive criticism without defending yourself.
- Refrain from talking too often or interrupting others.
- Request feedback.
- Express your needs, desires, or feelings without criticizing or blaming.

Verbal Communications with Customers: If you spend a lot of time communicating with consumers face-to-face, having the "gift of gab" can come in handy, particularly if you work in sales. However, keep in mind that meetings should be based on understanding and meeting your customers' needs; leveraging your language skills to facilitate consultative dialogues would ensure constructive connections with customers.

In particular:

- Anticipate the concerns of others.
- Ask for clarification.
- Ask open-ended questions to stimulate dialogue.
- Calm irritated customers by acknowledging and listening to their concerns.

- Emphasize the benefits of a good, service, or plan to convince a person.
- Recognize nonverbal cues and react orally to confirm uncertainty, defuse frustration, and so on.

Verbal Communications for Presenters: Public speaking is a skill that can be honed with practice and academic preparation. Speaking clearly and persuasively in front of a live audience should involve:

- Pronouncing every word you say clearly
- Introducing emphasis on the topic at the beginning of a presentation or conversation.
- Scheduling messages before you speak.
- Projecting your voice to fill the room.
- Providing concrete examples to illustrate the points.
- Summarizing key points made by other speakers.
- Supporting statements with facts and evidence.
- Tailoring messages to different audiences.
- Telling stories to capture audiences.
- Using humor to engage the audience.
- Recaping important points toward the end of a speech.
- Selecting the appropriate language for your audience.
- Speaking at a moderate pace, not too fast or too slow.
- Speaking with confidence and modesty.

CHARACTERISTICS OF AN EFFECTIVE VERBAL COMMUNICATOR

Attributes of an effective communicator include:

- Active Listening.
- Adaptability: adapt your communication styles to support the situation.
- Clarity.
- Confidence and Assertiveness.
- Constructive feedback: give it and receive it.
- Emotional intelligence: recognizing and controlling feelings, as well as the emotions of others.
- Empathy.
- Interpersonal skills: social skills particularly useful for establishing close bonds.
- Body language interpretation, this will help you understand how someone is feeling.
- Open-mindedness.
- Patience.
- Simplify the complex.
- Narrative.

TECHNIQUES FOR IMPROVING VERBAL COMMUNICATION

Communication is a skill that can be developed and improved. Here are some strategies to help you develop your skills.

THE POWER OF THE MIND

Sometimes we talk while we think, but this can undermine our reputation because what we are doing is normally unhelpful and projects us as anxious people. Most of the presentation is about being still, listening and responding thoughtfully.

When answering questions and conversing, keep the following formula in mind and answer simply, directly, and concisely:

- Think
- Breathe
- Talk

So instead of saying the first thing that comes to mind, be thoughtful and focus on the essence and what you want to share. Understand the message you are trying to convey during the conversation. If you're not confident in your presentation, your audience won't be as a result either.

POSITIVE VISUALIZATION

Athletes use this strategy before a race; they visualize themselves competing and focus deeply on this thought. This gives them a motivational boost, which turns into physical benefits.

You will use this approach before a large presentation by seeing yourself standing with a microphone in front of hundreds of people, delivering your speech while the crowd seems interested, then ending your speech while the audience applauds.

Exercise - Positive visualization

- Find a quiet place to sit and relax.
- Close your eyes.
- Think of a time when you felt confident in yourself. It can be anything: a personal achievement, a childhood memory, or a fruitful work assignment. Take yourself back there and repeat the sequence of events.
- Be as detailed as possible in reliving your chosen moment.
- Listen to sounds and feel emotions.
- Repeat this process a few times until you are immersed in the event.
- Now open your eyes.

This is a perfect technique to use during a presentation and can help you calm your anxiety and boost your morale.

KEEP YOUR AUDIENCE IN MIND

To successfully connect, you must first understand your audience. Through this understanding, you'll tailor your correspondence to their needs, ensuring that your message has the greatest effect possible.

To improve this skill, imagine yourself in the audience's shoes; consider their demographics and shared characteristics. Inquire about why they are there. What do they want to know. What kind of skills and experience do they have.

Above all, it develops Empathy.

Empathy involves the ability to identify and understand someone's thoughts, for example by imagining yourself in that person's shoes. Understanding how others feel will help you express your opinions and ideas in a way that makes sense to you, as well as understanding others when they communicate.

To Develop Empathi

Put yourself in someone else's shoes. And if you have not been in a comparable position, remember a time when you had the same emotions as your colleague/friend.

Observe your colleagues, and try to understand how they are. Never ignore the emotions of those around you; for example, if someone is angry, don't ignore them; rather, help them.

Rather than passing judgement, try to understand first. For example, you may be initially irritated by a cold and disinterested colleague. However, once you understand that they suffer from social anxiety, you may become more compassionate.

To express your empathy and in demonstrating your honesty, keep your body language open, your voice under control and your breathing deep.

EFFECTIVE CENTRING AND POSTURE

When an individual is centred, he or she is balanced and at ease. Getting used to centring your energy on your centre of gravity will help you maintain an open, relaxed posture to make room for deeper, more fluid breaths. Feel the weight of your body on your heels. Keep your head up.

Consider the region halfway between your front and back body, just behind your waist. Stand with your feet shoulder-width apart and your arms free along your sides. Try to focus your energy more on this centre before a big meeting or presentation; it will increase your presence and catapult you into the critical moment.

USING THE FULL CAPACITY OF YOUR VOICE

The human voice can produce 24 notes on a musical scale. In a daily conversation, we only use three. Consider this the next time you speak, as expanding your vocabulary would help you easily improve your communication skills. This will serve to enthuse, convince and excite the individual or people you are talking to.

When your breath brings oxygen to your vocal cords, sound echoes in your lungs. Your tongue shapes and manipulates the sound, providing us with voice, tone, and accent.

The more oxygen you have in your lungs, the better the sounds will echo, allowing you to hear a greater variety of audible voices. Most of us use less than a third of our vocal capacity, which is normally due to precarious use of proper breathing.

BREATHE DEEPLY TO COMMUNICATE EFFECTIVELY

You breathe every time you dream. You breathe every time you speak. Since we breathe unconsciously, we don't think about it at all when we talk. When we are stressed, our breathing becomes shallow. Since this is combined with the overly long sentences that normally follow speech, words tend to fade out towards the end.

It is important to maximize your breath and fill your lungs during communication to develop strong communication skills. It will make you look stronger.
Remember to pause for emphasis, take a breath, and let the message sink in.

CHAPTER 14
<u>LEARN TO ASK</u>

If you ask the wrong questions, you will almost certainly get the wrong answers, or at least one that is not exactly what you are looking for.

The ability to ask the right question is critical to good dialogue and knowledge sharing. You can develop a wide variety of leadership skills by asking the right questions at the right time. For example, you will gain more knowledge and understand more, develop closer relationships, organize others more efficiently, and help others learn as well.

In this part, we'll look at some traditional query strategies and when to use them (and when not to).

OPEN AND CLOSED QUESTIONS

Normally a closed-ended question is answered with one word or a very short, truthful answer. *"Are you thirsty?"* for example. *"Yes" or "No"* is usually the answer; *"Where do you live?"* In most cases, the answer is the name of your town or your address.

Longer answers are elicited by open-ended questions. They typically begin with what, when, and how. An open-ended question elicits information, perspective, or emotions from the respondent. *"Tell me"* and *"describe"* should be used in the same way as open-ended questions.

HERE ARE A FEW EXAMPLES:

- *What happened at the meeting?*

- *Why did you react that way?*
- *Tell me what happened next.*
- *Tell the situation more precisely.*

Open-Ended questions are useful for:
- Initiating an interactive discussion, *"What did you do on vacation?"*
- Getting more information, *"What else do we need to do to make it productive?"*
- Finding out the other person's perspective or concerns: *"What do you think about these changes?"*

Closed-Ended questions are good for:

- Testing your (or the other person's) interpretation, *"Does this mean I will get a raise if I meet this requirement?"*
- Coming to a conclusion or making a decision, *"Now that we have all the evidence, do we all agree that this is the best course of action?"*
- Establishing the frame, *"Are you satisfied with your bank's service?"*

A badly asked closed question, on the other hand, will ruin the dialogue and lead to uncomfortable silences.

FILTERED QUESTIONS

This method involves starting with general questions and then narrowing the field with more specific requests. Typically, this would involve asking for more and more information. When the police receive a statement from a witness, they often use the following phrases:

- *"How many people were involved in the fight?"*
- *"About ten."*
- *"Were they children or adults?"*
- *"Mostly children."*
- *"How old were they?"*
- *"About fourteen or fifteen years."*
- *"Were any of them wearing anything distinctive?"*
- *"Yes, many of them had red baseball caps."*
- *"Do you remember if there was a logo on one of the caps?"*
- *"Now that you ask, yes, I remember seeing a big letter N."*

The detective used this method to assist the witness in reliving the scene and ultimately focusing on a valuable detail. He would not have had this information if he had asked an open-ended question such as *"Are there any details you can give me about what you saw?"*

Start with closed questions using the filtered interview. As you progress, start asking more open-ended questions.

Filtered Questions are useful for:

- Getting more information on a given point: *"Can you tell me more about Option Two?"*

- Increasing the curiosity or confidence of the person you are talking to: *"Did you contact the IT helpdesk?" "Did it solve your problem?" "What did the person who answered your call say?"*

SURVEY QUESTIONS

Another method of getting more information is to ask probing questions. Often what you need to do is ask your respondent for an analogy to help you clarify a comment they have created.

Sometimes more detail is needed for clarity, such as *"What do you need this report for, do you want to see a draft before I send you my final version?"* Or to see if there is evidence for what was said, *"How do you know the current database can't be used by the sales department?"*

A good probing technique will help you get to the bottom of a dilemma easily.

To get more information, ask questions that contain the word "exactly": *"What exactly do you mean by fast track?"* or *"Who, exactly, wanted this report?"*

Survey Questions are useful for:
- Get clarity to ensure you have a complete understanding of the speech.
- Get information from people who avoid asking you anything.
- Tendentious questions.

PERSUASIVE QUESTIONS

Persuasive questions attempt to persuade the respondent of your point of view. They will do this in a variety of ways:

- With a hypothetical, *"How soon do you think the proposal will be delivered?"* This means that the project will almost inevitably not be finished on schedule.
- Adding a personal plea to agree at the end: *"Don't you think Luca is really good?"* or *"Isn't the second option better?"*
- Formulating the question so that the simplest answer is a "yes." Our innate preference to say "yes" rather than "no" plays an important role in the wording of the question: *"Do we all approve option two?"* is more likely to elicit a favorable response than *"Do you want to approve option two or not?"*
- Giving people a choice between two options. You will be satisfied with both, it will be better than choosing between one option or not choosing at all. When asked, *"Which would you choose ... A or B?"* the choice "neither" is always possible, but most people are more likely to choose one of your two options.

It's worth noting that persuasive questions are usually close-ended.

Persuasive Questions are useful for:

- Getting the desired response thus leaving the other person with the impression that they have no choice.
- Closing a sale: *"If this solves all your questions, can we agree on a price?"*
-

Be careful when asking important questions. If you ask them in a way that is selfish or detrimental to the other person's needs, you will be seen as misleading and deceptive.

RHETORICAL QUESTIONS

Rhetorical questions aren't really questions, so you don't expect an answer. They are really just comments phrased in the form of questions, *"Is it true that John's work is very creative?"*

People use rhetorical questions when engaging the audience, prompting them to agree, *"Yes, he is, and I'd love to collaborate with such a good colleague."* Rather than saying things like *"Marco is a really creative artist."* (To which they might respond, *"So what?"*).

When you use a series of rhetorical questions, they become even more effective. *"Isn't this a show? Don't you simply love how the text picks up the colors in the photos? Doesn't it make good use of space? Wouldn't it be great if we could get a show like this for our products?"*

Rhetorical Questions are useful for the following purposes:
- Engage the listener.
- Getting people to agree with your point of view.

QUESTIONS ARE A POWERFUL WAY TO:

- **Learn:** Use open and closed-ended questions as well as survey questions.

- **Establish relationships:** People normally respond favorably when asked what they do or what their opinions are. If you respond affirmatively, such as, "Tell me what you like best about your work here", you will help develop and maintain an open dialogue.

- **Manage and coach**: Rhetorical and guided questions are also helpful in this situation. They should encourage people to think and look inside themselves.
- **Avoid misunderstandings:** Use interrogative questions to gain clarity, particularly when the stakes are high. Also, be sure not to jump to conclusions.
- **Calm a Hot Situation:** You'll calm an angry customer or colleague by asking filtered questions to get more information about their request. Not only will this distract them from their feelings, but it can often help you identify one small tangible thing you can do, which is often enough to make them feel like they've "earned" something and no longer deserve to be annoyed.
- **Persuade People:** No one likes to be lectured to, but asking a series of open-ended questions will get you to accept the reasoning behind your point of view. *"What do you think about calling the sales department on the computer for a half-day update?"*

Allow enough time for the person you are interviewing to respond. Generally some time is needed, so do not simply interpret a delay as 'no answer'.

A skilful interview must be accompanied by careful listening to learn what people really mean while they are answering. When you ask questions, body language and tone of voice will also influence the answers you get.

CHAPTER 15
HOW TO HANDLE NEGATIVE OPINIONS AND CRITICISM

Has your day been ruined by an impertinent remark or unwelcome feedback? If so, you are not alone; criticism affects many people and denotes an evaluation or decision, either positive or negative depending on particular criteria. It has an effect on our ideals.

You should, nevertheless, prevent opponents from infiltrating your magnificence with their remarks. You should also use criticism to improve yourself. Your professional and personal success is determined by your ability to accept feedback of any kind.

The modern world is not full of self-esteem. It only takes the slightest of negative reviews at work or a sassy message on an Instagram post to completely derail your day.

It may take a lot of time and resources to convince you that you are exceptional, but how can we prevent outsiders from infiltrating to ruin your self-esteem? And how can we improve?

Anyone who has ever been transported to a YouTube, Facebook or Instagram comments section will be able to attest that living in our digital age means being bombarded by waves of feedback, both online and offline.

However, criticism is essential. Personal and career outcomes both depend on the ability to accept feedback calmly. The desire to actually listen and understand the thoughts of others, especially if they are negative, strengthens relationships, academic success, and negotiation skills.

Moreover, if you learn to silence your pride and also use candid feedback to improve, you will have a strong weapon that will carry you forward both socially and professionally.

This section will teach you how to deal with what people say without having to crawl into a corner or get angry at someone. The word criticism indicates a positive or negative evaluation and is ubiquitous. When someone criticises you, they are judging you according to clear criteria, whether their own or those of an organisation such as a workplace. Students and workers often equate the term 'criticism' with exclusively negative reviews, but this is not the case.

THERE ARE MANY REASONS WHY PEOPLE CRITICIZE.

Reasons that lead to negative criticism might include jealousy or insecurity in a marital or family relationship, such as a father blaming his children for never calling home. Others may condemn you simply out of spite.

However, not all feedback is negative and very often you will need it to evolve and improve, the important thing is that it does not overtly and negatively highlight errors and deficiencies.

This is because certain types of criticism are provided to help. This is known as constructive criticism.

A 2018 study used focus group interviews with college students to assess patterns of positive criticism.

This study established three essential conditions for negative criticism to be constructive:

- **They are Compassionate**: Criticism should come from people close to you and offer advice in a way that shows concern for the recipient.
- **They are Specific:**   The critique should focus on relevant aspects of the recipient's results and include concrete suggestions for change.
- **They are Reciprocal:** Criticism should be directed at the feelings and motivations of the recipient.

You will use this list to decide if a person is trying to support you or hurt you.

HOW TO DEAL WITH CRITICISM WITHOUT DAMAGING YOUR SELF-ESTEEM

1. HONESTLY EVALUATE THE CRITIC'S INTENTION.

Since no one is excluded, listen critically to negative comments. Thinking about your strengths and weaknesses will help you approach criticism with an open mind and recognize the difference. Someone may order you, for example, to politely drink your coffee or return to your desk. At first glance, the remark may seem confrontational. However, if you reason calmly, you may see that the individual may be struggling with personal issues. This means that they are not in conflict with you as a person.

2. DETERMINE WHETHER THE FEEDBACK PROVIDED IS CONSTRUCTIVE OR DESTRUCTIVE

Before making any decisions, you need to evaluate a number of factors. Did the person providing the input understand how to care for you by advising you how to proceed?

An authoritative individual, might criticize your work and then use self-aggrandizing or demeaning language. Such a person drags you into an endless race for dominance.

So, respond according to the intent of the critique and after considering those close to you. Consider their comment as a discussion and, if you disagree, let them know.

3. SHOWS APPRECIATION FOR THOSE WHO OFFER CONSTRUCTIVE CRITICISM

Thank anyone who gives you constructive feedback; they only want what is good for you. Although it may be annoying to realise what you did wrong, consider their motives and thank them.

4. WHEN DEALING WITH CONSTRUCTIVE CRITICISM, KEEP YOUR EMOTIONS IN CHECK.

Avoid blowing up when you receive feedback, even though it is clearly damaging. You shouldn't respond angrily to comments, as you will surely regret it later.

Don't let others damage your self-esteem. Then, look for an explanation and you'll find that most negative remarks will thin out like smoke. Ultimately, it's always a good idea to put your feelings aside and take a deep breath before responding.

5. *APOLOGIZE FOR YOUR WEAKNESS*

An apology shows that you are willing to accept responsibility instead of avoiding it. It also changes the scenario from a combative one to a collaborative one. This also helps change the considerations of the opposing side.

6. *CONSIDER SUGGESTIONS, NOT THE TONE OF THE FEEDBACK*

Understand that some people may provide helpful comments, but their tone and manner of speaking may interfere with how you receive them. To that end, it is best to respond in a calm rather than confrontational manner. So, separate the two and focus on the helpful suggestions.

7. *AVOID TAKING CRITICISM PERSONALLY*

When people are criticized, they also feel personally attacked. They see it as an assault on their ego. It is important to recognize that often, there is a tendency to criticize the envy or pride of others, which is simply a fleeting feeling and not the true essence of a person.

8. *SMILE*

Put on a smile and you'll feel at ease. A smile will make you feel better and lighten the mood. As a result, this will benefit you socially and inspire the other person to be more moderate in their approach.

9. *ACTING ON POSITIVE FEEDBACK*

Create mechanisms to focus on the topics that have received the most attention in reviews. It is important to recognize that most opponents are right in some way.

Therefore, especially if the criticism is severe, make sure you have learnt something.

10. SILENCE THE CRITIC.

You may need to calm naysayers from time to time by reminding them that you realize you haven't met their needs, but that you can still do better next time.
Time will help them manage how they provide input in the future.

11. INFORM THEM THAT YOU ARE UNABLE TO LISTEN AT THIS TIME.

If you can't listen, don't feel guilty about withdrawing from a conversation. Let the person know that you enjoy conversing with them, but now is not the time. Then proceed to suggest an appropriate time to resume the discussion. This move will allow them to rethink or weigh their criticism, making it more concrete.

12. SPEAK YOUR SIDE OF THE STORY.

Inform the one you are talking to of your thoughts on the topic. It is crucial to keep peace with people; however, being too cooperative to avoid confrontation at all costs is not the only way out. You should express yourself tactfully and at the right time. So, speak up while you have the opportunity to be heard, because even harsh arguments can be expressed.

13. BE COMPASSIONATE WITH YOURSELF.

When you receive negative criticism, be kind to yourself. Give yourself a gift and start a constructive dialogue. Tell yourself that although the criticism is annoying, it does not characterize you.

14. RELEASE YOUR FEELINGS.

Sometimes feeling hurt or upset is unavoidable and hiding your feelings is counterproductive. As a result, express your thoughts or handwrite them; either way, express them creatively and move on.

15. REDUCE YOUR CONTACT WITH NEGATIVE PEOPLE.

You can sever relationships with people who have a habit of providing negative feedback. It is time to forge your own identity by severing ties with these people.

In life you will receive positive and negative reviews from family, friends, and employers. However, you can effectively absorb criticism by determining its intent, listening quietly, acting on comments, and breaking ties with negative people. As a result, to live a happy life, it is important to learn how to respond to and filter feedback.

CHAPTER 16
ANXIETY AND STRESS MANAGEMENT

Stress affects almost everyone at some point in their lives. This is the body's response to something that has happened or is currently happening. Your body responds to the condition by causing physical, behavioral or emotional stress.

Stress is very common, but it doesn't have to be a bad thing. In fact, stress is one of the ways the body helps us avoid risk. It can also increase efficiency and inspiration. Positive life changes, such as a move, a new job, a wedding or a new baby, can also trigger stress.

Although stress has some benefits, chronic or severe stress is a completely different story and can can have a negative effect on your health and lifestyle. Anticipating a stressful event can induce tension and anxiety in some people. Chronic stress will make people feel like they are negatively affected at all times and in every decision they make. This form of stress and anxiety is harmful and can lead to serious physical, behavioural or emotional problems.

One of the most effective ways to combat stress in the long term is to learn how to manage it safely. Stress management is the most important element in gaining self-confidence. Lifestyle is an interesting term because it includes so many ideas, but to me it means having the freedom to change what you want in your life, both personal and professional, by taking control of your emotions and your destiny.

We will now explain, the consequences of stress, how it affects communication and the best ways to deal with it.

EFFECTS OF STRESS

When the body reacts to stress several things will happen. Your heart rate will accelerate, your blood pressure will increase, your breathing will become faster, and your muscles will stiffen. This is referred to as the "run or fight" response. If possible, the body prepares to respond quickly.
Stress can cause symptoms that spread throughout your entire being. It can cause physical, social and behavioral problems if it is severe or permanent.

STRESS SYMPTOMS

When under stress, the body reacts in a variety of ways.

Physical Symptoms are as follows:

- Stomach upset, diarrhea, constipation, nausea.
- Muscle aches, pains, tension.
- Insomnia or other sleep problems.
- Energy Loss.
- Headaches.
- Nervousness or tremor.
- Lowered immune system.
- Dry Mouth.
- Clenched Jaw.
- Hyperventilation.
- Sweating.

Prolonged stress can also lead to heart failure, elevated blood pressure and irregular heartbeats. Stress can cause heart attacks or strokes and can also contribute to panic attacks that mimic a heart attack.

Obesity, eating habits, menstrual disorders, and respiratory infections can all be caused by long-term stress.

Stress can cause skin problems such as acne, psoriasis, eczema and hair loss.
Irritable bowel syndrome, peptic ulcer and gastroesophageal reflux disease can also be caused by the effects of stress on the digestive tract.

Emotional and Mental symptoms of Stress

Stress doesn't just affect your physical body, it can also affect your emotional and mental state.

Here are some common ways a person can experience emotional distress due to stress:

- Moodiness or irritability.
- Low Self-Esteem.
- Depression.
- Anxiety.
- Avoiding other people.
- Feeling overwhelmed.
- Overconcern.

Prolonged stress can be extremely detrimental to a person's mental and emotional health.

The field of study known as psychoneuroimmunology (PNI) investigates the relationship between the immune system and the body's nervous system. According to MentalHelp.net, "PNI research suggests that chronic stress can lead to exacerbating mood disorders such as depression and anxiety, bipolar disorder, cognitive (thinking) problems, personality changes, and problem behaviors.

HOW STRESS AFFECTS COMMUNICATION AND HOW TO MANAGE IT

Communication is another way in which tension is expressed. People who are stressed are more likely to become angry or nervous. This will have a negative impact on the ability to communicate. When a person's emotions are at their highest, they may have difficulty carefully selecting words or expressing themselves appropriately.

Public speaking is another area where stress can have an effect on communication. For some, fear of public speaking prevents them from standing up in front of an audience. Stress can be harmful to some individuals in various ways, but it can also be regulated.

IDENTIFICATION OF CAUSES OF STRESS

One of the first steps in stress management is to determine the primary source. You may not always be aware of what is causing your discomfort. You may be under a lot of stress without knowing what it is due to.

These are also known as "causes of stress." Not everyone is bothered by the same problem. One individual may be stressed by work or school, while another may be embarrassed in social settings. Everyone has something unique that can trigger their stress response.
Once you've identified the factors, you'll begin to control the agitation and come up with a concrete approach to combat it.

INCREASE COMMUNICATION WITH THOSE AROUND YOU

When we communicate poorly with others, our stress levels skyrocket as well.

There are times in our lives when no one can help us with our stress load. However, there are times when we can reduce our tension by conversing.

Here are some ways you can use touch and communication to reduce stress.

1. COMMUNICATING IN WORK AND ACADEMIA

Work is a huge source of depression for many people. When you start a new career, you expect your stress levels to increase as you learn to complete new tasks. However, if you've been working for a long time and your employer has unreasonable ambitions, it may be time to talk about it. A safe work environment requires effective communication.

While it is not necessary to have a communicative relationship with your supervisor, it is preferable to suffering under extreme stress. Your employer may not lighten the load, but they may have innovative solutions to help you succeed.

Students are no exception. If the topic you are covering is too complicated, contact your professor. They will notice that you are actually making an attempt and will be willing to find you a tutor or provide assistance.

2. COMMUNICATE IN RELATIONSHIPS

Relationships with others are another common cause of stress. Relationships and social support are critical to a person's well-being. When pressures with a girlfriend, roommate, family member or close friend are high, our stress levels will skyrocket.

Early communication is one way to stop strained relationships. Instead of waiting until you reach a breaking point, communicate to a friend, relative, or loved one what is irritating you. You'll reduce potentially tense scenarios by politely expressing anger or dissatisfaction.
Likewise, we should be prepared to listen to how someone close to us, shares their emotions.

3. *TALK ABOUT STRESS WITH FRIENDS, FAMILY AND LOVED ONES*

If you are overwhelmed or frustrated with life, talk to someone. Talk to others about the things that are causing you discomfort and the feelings you are experiencing.
If you suffer from chronic depression, you should seek the assistance of a licensed physician to help you relieve the stress. In fact, communicating our feelings and putting our emotions in writing will reduce the intensity of depression, anger and pain and help us feel better more quickly.

OTHER WAYS TO REDUCE STRESS

Eating well is also believed to help reduce stress. Beverages containing caffeine, when drunk in large quantities, can have a toxic impact on the body and increase stress. The same can be said for excessive consumption of alcohol, sugar, salt and nicotine.

Foods rich in vitamin B, vitamin C and magnesium can help relieve stress. When you're stressed, these nutrients will help your body regain energy and strength.

Getting enough sleep, meditating, praying and doing relaxing things like a hot bath or massage will also help. Another way to significantly relieve depression is to take up a hobby or outdoor activity.

Although stress is an inevitable part of life, it does not have to overwhelm you. If you are stressing yourself out every day, start by making small adjustments that will make you feel better. These small changes can be the beginning of a real transformation, freeing you from the burden of stress.

COMMUNICATION (PUBLIC SPEAKING) ANXIETY AND HOW TO DEAL WITH IT

When a person has to speak in front of an audience, he or she suffers from communication anxiety. Communication anxiety is a real pathology, particularly when you are expected to speak to groups as part of your job.

Men and women have different communication styles, but they all have one thing in common that causes communication anxiety: a loss of trust. Regardless of what caused the loss of trust, the individual suffering from communication anxiety fears that something will go terribly wrong during the conversation and that they will not be able to recover properly.

An increased heart rate, sweating, loss of concentration, and dry mouth are just some of the typical symptoms of plenary communication anxiety. Cognitive behavioral therapy (CBT) or tranquilizers can help with this type of anxiety, but there are also things you can do on your own to train yourself to speak up in difficult situations.

Recognize that you suffer from communication anxiety and make an effort to take action to improve the condition. First, if necessary, avoid meetings with a hostile audience.
If you are called upon to speak in the near future, here are some other things you could do:

Prepare for the challenge. Being in front of a group of people is stressful enough; not understanding what you are talking about will only complicate the situation. Preparation will go a long way in alleviating fear and apprehension in communication.

Get your mind to accept the task. Visualize yourself speaking in front of an audience. Examine your appearance. Take a look at the crowd. Perceive familiar feelings and allow your brain to develop confidence. Once your mind is involved in the context, it will help you stay calm when you speak.
Recognize that you have anxiety about speaking and anticipate the signs that will appear as you prepare to communicate. That way, you are not caught off guard.

Breathe deeply and be patient as you begin. If you can hold on for a few minutes, your heart rate may decrease and other symptoms may subside.
Remember not to overcompensate for your fear. Inform the crowd that you are excited. Also try to look happy; this can

help drain your nervous energy by giving the crowd the impression that you are excited. People will understand your intentions if they sense calmness and enthusiasm rather than anxiety and fear.

Focus on the present moment. Don't let your thoughts wander to the future, imagining possible scenarios. Stay in the present, where you have the power to act.

CHAPTER 17

ANGER MANAGEMENT

The inability to control frustration will lead to many problems, such as saying something you will later regret, yelling at your children, bullying co-workers, sending reckless letters, having poor health, and even resorting to physical abuse. However, not all cases are extreme.

Anger can come in many forms, including: wasting time worrying about annoying activities, getting frustrated with traffic, or lashing out at work.

Managing dismay does not mean never being angry again. Instead, it involves learning to understand, cope with, and articulate outrage in positive and constructive ways.

Everyone should learn to control their anger. Even if you think you have mastered the art of anger management, there is still room for growth. Because uncontrolled frustration can often lead to destructive actions, anger management employs a variety of approaches to help an individual manage emotions, feelings, and attitudes in a safe and constructive way.

Anger is a normal, balanced feeling that is neither positive nor negative. Like any other emotion, it conveys a message, informing you that a situation is disturbing, unfair, or dangerous.

However, if the first reaction to outrage is to explode, the message will never be communicated. Although it is natural to be angry when you have been mistreated or wronged, outrage becomes troubling when you display it in a way that hurts yourself or others.

You may believe that expressing anger is good, that people around you are too emotional, that anger is justified, or that you need to show it to get respect.

However, the fact is that indignation is likely to have a detrimental effect on the way others see you, hindering your progress.

EFFECTS OF ANGER

Chronic anger, which continually flares up or becomes uncontrollable, can have major consequences for you:

- **Physical Health.** Consistently working at high levels of stress and anger increases the risk of heart disease, diabetes, a compromised immune system, anxiety and high blood pressure.

- **Mental Health.** Chronic anger weakens your emotional capacity and blurs your vision, making it hard to focus or enjoy life. It can cause fatigue, depression and other mental health problems.

- **Career.** Constructive criticism and heated discussion can both be beneficial. However, getting angry only alienates your colleagues, bosses, or clients, eroding their esteem.

- **Relationships**. Anger will leave lasting scars on the people you care about most, as well as severing connections and working relationships. Explosive anger makes it difficult for someone to believe you, speak freely, or feel comfortable, and is especially harmful to children.

If you have a fiery temperament, you may feel like you have little control over yourself and there is nothing you can do to calm yourself down. However, you have more decision-making power than you think. You can learn to show your feelings without offending people and keep your temper from taking over your life if you understand the real triggers behind your frustration and use these anger control techniques.

ANGER MYTHS AND FACTS

Myth: You don't have to "contain" anger. It is helpful to vent and get it all out.
Fact: Anger is not something that needs to be 'released' aggressively in order to feel better. Outbursts and shouting, on the other hand, simply add fuel to the fire and reinforce the quarrel.

Myth: Anger, violence, and coercion help you get recognition and what you want.
Fact: Bullying others does not create respect. People will fear you, and they won't appreciate you since you can't hold back and deal with different points of view. If you interact in a friendly way, others will be more likely to listen to you and meet your needs.

Myth: It is not possible to improve. Anger is uncontrollable.
Fact: You can't really control how you feel or the situation you are in, but you can control how you convey your anger. You should also express emotions without being verbally or physically abusive. And if someone is bothering you, you have the ability to control how you react.

ANGER MANAGEMENT E STRATEGIES

Anger is a powerful emotion that can range from moderate irritation to pure wrath. Although many people consider outrage purely a "negative feeling," it can also be constructive. Feelings of anger can motivate you to support others or implement social change.

However, uncontrolled anger can lead to violent actions such as yelling at others or destroying objects. Feelings of anger will also cause you to withdraw into yourself and focus your anger inward, which can have a negative effect on your health and well-being.

Anger becomes a challenge when it is felt too often or too strongly, or when it is manifested in inappropriate ways and can negatively impact your physical, emotional, and social well-being. As a result, conflict control tools can be helpful in helping you discover safe ways to share your emotions.

ANGER MANAGEMENT STRATEGIES

Cognitive-behavioral therapies have shown in several cases to be successful in improving fight control. These treatments include altering thinking and behavior. They are based on the idea that your perceptions, emotions, and actions are all connected.

Your feelings and actions will either increase or decrease your emotions. So, if you want to remove anger from your mental state, you should change what you say and do. Without oxygen, the fire inside you will continue to diminish and you will feel more comfortable.

Creating an anger management strategy is the only way to manage conflict. If you feel frustrated you will know how to act.

Here are some tactics to consider when using your anger management strategy. These techniques are intended to help you manage and control your emotions.

IDENTIFY TRIGGERS

Make a list of the things that make you angry if you've developed the habit of losing your temper. Long lines, traffic congestion, irreverent tweets, and exhaustion are just a few of the factors that can make you lose your cool.

While you can't blame someone or something for your inability to stay calm, knowing what causes your anger will help you prepare accordingly.

You can plan to restructure your day to better manage stress. Alternatively, you could practice some conflict control exercises before you encounter situations that normally upset you. These actions will help you stretch the fuse, which means that a single frustrating episode won't set you off.

ASSESS YOUR ANGER

Before taking steps to calm yourself down, consider whether your outrage is towards a friend or a hostile adversary.

In these situations, you may want to change the condition, rather than your emotional state. Anger may be a warning sign that something else needs to change, such as an emotionally manipulative relationship or a dysfunctional friendship.

Being angry will give you the confidence you need to take a stand or make a change.

If, on the other hand, your indignation was causing you pain or damaging your relationships, it could be a big problem Feeling out of control and later regretting your comments or behaviors are both symptoms of this form of anger. Under these circumstances, it makes sense to focus on dealing with your feelings and calming down.

RECOGNIZE DANGER SIGNS

As is often the case with many people, you may feel anger come out of nowhere. You may go from calm to angry in an instant. However, there are always warning signs to indicate that frustration is building. Recognizing them early will help you take action and prevent your frustration from exploding and spilling over.

Consider the physical symptoms of indignation you may be experiencing. Perhaps your heart rate has increased or your face has become hot. Or maybe you start to clench your fists. Maybe your mind begins to race or you start to "see black."

By knowing the warning signs, you will be able to take decisive action to avoid doing or performing anything that could cause bigger problems. Pay attention to how you feel and you will improve your ability to see the warning signs.

BACK OFF

Trying to win an argument or staying in an unfavorable situation will only fuel your anger. When your frustration grows, one of the safest things you can do is to distance yourself from the situation if possible.

When an argument gets heated, take a break and if you think you're going to blow up retreat and avoid confrontation. A break can be very helpful in calming both your mind and body.

When you need a break, make it clear that you're not trying to avoid difficult topics, just that you're focusing on anger management. When you're angry, it's hard to have a constructive conversation or resolve a disagreement. When you feel more relaxed, you are able to address the conversation and bring up the topic again.

This gives your spouse, colleague or family member peace of mind that the issue will be addressed, at a later date.

TALK TO A FRIEND

Talking about a problem or sharing your emotions with someone who is able to calm you down can be helpful. However, it is important to remember that complaining about this or that, listing all the reasons you don't like others, or grumbling about all the injustices you feel can intensify anger. However, studies suggest that it is not necessary to "vent your frustration." Smashing things when you're angry, for example, can make you even angrier. As a result, it is important to be careful when using this strategy.

Similarly, if you're going to talk to a friend, make sure you reduce your anger rather than lashing out. It's unfair to use them as dummies. Instead, you may find that, the easiest way to get the anger through is to talk about something other than the situation that is driving you crazy.

MOVE

Anger causes outbursts of anger. Exercise is one of the easiest ways to make the most of this energy. Working out, whether it's a brisk walk or a session at the gym, will help you de-stress.

Daily activity also helps with the decompression process. Aerobic exercise reduces discomfort, which can help you manage anger better. Exercise also helps you clear your head. You'll find that after a long run or strenuous exercise, you'll have a better understanding of what was bothering you.

MANAGE YOUR THOUGHTS

Feelings of anger add fuel to the flames. Thinking things like "I can't take it anymore. This traffic will ruin everything," will only cause more anger. Recreate your emotions when you notice yourself worrying about things that cause anger.

Try focusing on reality by combatting that thought with, "Every day, millions of cars are on the road. From time to time there will be road delays." Focusing on tolerance and understanding, without making dire predictions or immense exaggerations, will help you stay calm when situations arise. You can even create a mantra that you can repeat to block the emotions that are fueling your anger. Saying, "I'm fine", "Stay still", or "No need" repeatedly will help you mitigate or suppress feelings of anger.

CHANGE FILES IN YOUR MIND

Anger is fueled by dwelling on an irritating situation. If you had a difficult day at work, for example, going over everything that went wrong will leave you frustrated.

Changing files in your mind and focusing on something else, could be the perfect way to relax.

It's not always possible to say to yourself, "Don't worry about it." Distracting yourself by taking active action is the perfect way to physically shift gears. Do something that demands your full attention and makes it harder for feelings of frustration and pessimism to enter your head.

Thoroughly cleaning the house, weeding the garden, playing with the kids, planting flowers, or painting a picture are just a few examples. Do enough to occupy your mind so you don't ruminate on the things that bother you. Then, both your body and your mind can relax.

There are several calming techniques that can be used to relieve frustration. The trick is to choose the one that works best for you. Breathing exercises and gradual muscle relaxation are two popular ways to reduce stress.

The best thing is that all the exercises can be completed easily and discreetly. So, if you're upset at work or annoyed about something, you can have the tension melt away quickly and easily.

It is important to remember, however, that relaxation techniques take practice. At first, you may not find them reliable or you may doubt that they work. Regardless, with practice, they will become fundamental exercises in anger management.

EXPLORE YOUR FEELINGS

It may be helpful to pause for a moment to consider what feelings might be hiding behind your outrage. Anger is often used as a defensive mask to save you from experiencing more negative feelings such as humiliation, depression, and disappointment.

When someone gives you harsh criticism, for example, you may explode in frustration because you feel humiliated. Convincing yourself that the other person is wrong to judge you might help you feel better by relieving your humiliation. However, remembering the underlying feelings will help you get to the source of the problem. Then, decide what steps to take.

For example, if someone cancels plans agreed upon with you and your underlying emotion is sadness, rather than lashing out in frustration, you might consider expressing how the situation makes you feel. When you are open about your emotions, you are more likely to find a solution. Responding with anger generally has the opposite effect and drives people away.

CREATE A "CALM DOWN" KIT

If you happen to come home from work exhausted and take out your frustration on your family, or if you know the office meeting is annoying you, put together a "calm down" kit that can help you relax.

Consider objects that can help you engage all of your senses. You'll change your mental state by looking, seeing, hearing, smelling and touching relaxing objects. A relaxation kit might contain a scented hand lotion, a picture of a peaceful landscape, a spiritual phrase to read aloud, or a couple of pieces of your favorite sweets. Bring objects with you that you know will help you remain calm.

You can even create a virtual relaxation kit that you can take with you wherever you go. There are more compact things you can use when you need them. Relaxing music and photos, guided meditation or instructions for breathing techniques, for example, can be saved in a special folder on your phone.

CONTROLLING ANGER USING COMMUNICATION SKILLS

Everyone gets angry from time to time, so if you can't handle the anger, you might do or say things without thinking, or even act violently by hurting people. Ignoring your emotions, on the other hand, will cause you to turn your frustration on yourself.
Using good listening skills to manage your outrage allows you to find a happy balance by learning to be assertive rather than abusive.

STEP 1

Calm yourself from the inside out before you say anything to anyone. Slow down your heart rate and calm your body using relaxation exercises. Use a particular expression to encourage yourself to relax, such as "Calm down" or "Relax." Remind yourself to listen before you respond and that being calm will allow you to assess the situation more accurately.

STEP 2

Consider the case objectively. Don't claim to "understand" how people feel or why they make certain decisions. Focus solely on the problem. Consider how the situation affects you so you can make rational decisions about how to deal with it.

This removes the emotional dimension and helps you to be more rational, helping to quell anger.

STEP 3

Respond assertively rather than violently. Use "I-phrases" rather than "you-phrases" to assert your needs.
 Use active listening techniques and make yourself collaborative but clearly state what is wrong with you.

STEP 4

Avoid overgeneralizations. Avoid using terms like "always," "never," or "everyone" in conversations.
This keeps the conversation focused on the topic at hand and prevents the anger from reaching unmanageable proportions.

STEP 5

Use nonverbal signals to convey assertiveness. Express various feelings in the way you express what you say. Use an authoritative tone of voice, stand up straight and look the other person in the eye. Maintain a neutral appearance with your mouth. Be careful with your hands. Don't make nervous or anxious movements, such as twisting your hands or biting your nails.
Monitoring your physical reactions will help you alleviate a stressful situation

CHAPTER 18
<u>STOP APOLOGIZING ALL THE TIME</u>

Apologizing means saying "I'm sorry" and is typically seen as an act of good. However, when you don't have to because you haven't done anything wrong or when you are accepting blame for someone else's mistake that you didn't cause or handle, it takes a different turn.

HERE ARE SOME EXAMPLES OF EXCESSIVE EXCUSES.

- When the waiter brings you the wrong order, you apologize and say, *"I'm sorry, but that's not what I ordered."*
- With the nurses in the outpatient clinic, *"I'm sorry to interrupt, I wanted to ask something."*
- The cashier at the store inadvertently breaks your eggs and you send someone to get another carton for you. You apologize to the people in line, saying, *"I'm sorry I wasted so much time."*
- Your partner makes a racist remark. *"Please excuse him. He's not normally like this,"* you tell your friends.
- You're in a meeting and you interrupt by saying, *"I'm sorry. I didn't understand what you meant. Could you please explain again what you just said?"*

WHY WE APOLOGIZE TOO MUCH AND WHY IT'S A PROBLEM

In all cases, it is obvious that you have done nothing wrong and there is no reason to apologize. So why do so many of us over-apologize?

The following are some potential reasons for this:

- **People's approval.** You want to be seen as a sweet and respectful individual. You are overly obsessed with what others think of you and don't want to offend or disappoint others.
- **Low Self-Esteem.** You have low self-esteem and, as a result, you are worried about doing something wrong, such as being strict, causing trouble, being irrational, or asking for too much.
- **Perfectionism.** You have such painfully high expectations of yourself that you will never reach them. As a result, you are constantly insecure and feel the need to apologize for every little thing you do incorrectly.
- **You feel uncomfortable.** We apologize when we are nervous or insecure and don't know what to do or say. As a result, we apologize to make ourselves or others feel better.
- **You hold yourself responsible for the mistakes or bad actions of others.** A partner in a relationship, for example, might apologize for the other person's actions (being late or interrupting) as if they themselves had done something wrong.
  This may be due to a lack of distinction, i.e. you behave as one entity rather than two separate individuals. You

are not responsible for the decisions of the people you are dating or married to. Taking responsibility and apologising for their actions simply encourages their problematic behaviour because you have absolved them of responsibility.

- **This is a bad habit.** If you've apologized too much or heard people apologize for too long, you may be doing it unintentionally. It's an unconscious reaction you make without even thinking about it. Too many good deeds aren't necessarily a good thing, and that goes for apologies as well. Excessively apologizing will alleviate the effect of your justifications when they are most required. Apologizing too much will also make you seem less optimistic. It can feel like you're sorry for everything: for your decisions and emotions, for taking up space, for being alive. This kind of insensitive apology is an indirect means of blaming yourself when it simply means repeating yourself, "I'm wrong" or "It's my fault." This does not indicate self-esteem or confidence.

- **Excessive apologizing is a common problem for people with codependent tendencies.** It is a sign of our low self-esteem, fear of confrontation, and a sharp emphasis on the desires and feelings of others. We also have weak boundaries, which are often intertwined with others; so we can take responsibility for actions we can't or shouldn't handle. We accept blame for trying to fix or overcome the concerns of others. We rationalize their behavior as if it were our own. We believe that everything is our fault, a belief that most likely has crept in from childhood. We are acutely aware that, in doing so, we become a burden. We are afraid of rejection and criticism, but we make every effort necessary to be accepted.

THINGS YOU SHOULD DEFINITELY STOP APOLOGIZING FOR.

Apologies are a natural part of life unless you're flawless (and no one is). And those two little words, "I'm sorry", have a lot of power.

An apology, according to research, relieves us of the shame of having wronged others and restores trust between the two parties.

They can also help us save face, become more accommodating to the opposing side, and build confidence in our own spiritual goodness and sympathy.

But, like so much sugar, too much "my fault" is bad.

Here are some common examples:

At a meeting, before you ask a question you say, *"I'm sorry, this is such a stupid thing to ask, but..."* or you interject by telling someone who bumps into you in the store, *"I'm sorry, I was in your way. I deeply apologize!"*

The older literature has shown this to be especially true for women. "Women who apologize a lot may be well-liked, but they are discarded for promotions because they don't seem good enough for the job," he says. "Then, once they avoid apologizing, they are judged to be too aggressive. "

According to Juliana Breines, Ph.D., assistant professor of psychology at the University of Rhode Island, excessive self-criticism may be to blame. "Excessive apologizing is due to being overly hard on ourselves, punishing ourselves for our wrongs, rather than accepting the fact that everyone makes mistakes and no one expects perfection."

She adds that when people feel ashamed or guilty, they may apologize to gain reassurance from others, even if the person they are apologizing to has not been hurt in any way by their actions. What is the end result? We risk feeding the mistaken belief that we are somehow guilty.

This, is not to diminish the importance of accepting our mistakes and making amends if we are wrong, but even if not, we say regardless, "I'm sorry."

Remember, there are many ways to relieve stress, be sympathetic to others, and show empathy other than using the words "I'm sorry."

WAYS TO STOP EXCESSIVE APOLOGIZING

While apologizing can be an effective way to promote loyalty and social stability, it is also important to be able to stand up for yourself and see yourself as capable of finding your own way in the world.

If you are constantly apologizing, you are sending a message to the universe that you are meek, uncertain, and undeserving. An unintentional "apology" has the ability to significantly reduce your capacity for manifestation. As a result, it shrinks you.

So how to do it?

1. PAUSE BEFORE APOLOGIZING.

Until you apologize, stop and ask yourself, *"Did I really do something wrong?"* Don't apologize if the answer is no! Temptation may be easier to suppress if you ask yourself, *"If I haven't done anything wrong, do I really want people to think I feel like I have?"*

2. KNOW YOUR TRIGGERS.

Have a short brainstorming session and write down the 10 reasons you feel you want to apologize. Consider what you might want to say instead of each reason. Spend a week focusing on just one of them, trying to remove the word "sorry" completely from context.

3. STRUCTURE THE QUESTIONS CAREFULLY.

When you need an explanation, it's not necessary to apologize too much, so don't. Instead, try asking questions like *"Could you explain more about this?"* or *"Could you help me understand more, maybe with an example?"*

4. TURN APOLOGIES INTO GRATITUDE.

Think of a way to rephrase your apology as a statement of thanks as often as needed. *"I'm sorry you had to run that errand,"* for example, can be quickly transformed into *"I'm so glad you did me this favor."* This is not only is more motivating for the listener, but it directs the mind to positivity and abundance. This will help you attract even more positivity.

Apologizing when we have obviously offended someone else, broken a law, or done something we think is wrong is a necessary step in restoring the social fabric that binds us to others. However, apologizing for something we are not responsible for not only invalidates us and reinforces feelings of low self-esteem, but it can also trivialize the process of apologizing and give people the idea that we are less competent.

It is difficult to abruptly change one's behavior. However, studies suggest that in some situations, not apologizing can be helpful. So, the next time you're tempted to apologize, take a deep breath, pause, and consider whether you're really to blame. If not, accept that you don't need to apologize.

CHAPTER 19
<u>BECOME ASSERTIVE</u>

As we approach the conclusion of this book, I would like to summarise the main concepts and leave you with some suggestions that will help you feel more comfortable defending yourself and fighting for yourself.

We would all like to be able to comfortably maintain our position and publicly share our opinions with those around us, whether it's turning down an offer or disagreeing with a colleague, a friend, a relative However, it's not easy.

When you're in the heat of the moment, it's hard to practice being assertive and it is helpful to improve emotionally with constructive inner dialogue.

It may sound trivial, but if you are about to have a conversation in which you know you will have to impose yourself, prepare yourself by thinking optimistic things like "I have to do this" or "My time is precious. "

If the mere thought of setting boundaries makes your heart rate increase, take a moment to breathe deeply, particularly if you feel aggression rising.

PRATICAL TIPS AND TECHNIQUES

DEEP BREATHING EXERCISE

Try this exercise the next time you feel unable to concentrate:
- Find a quiet place to sit or stand.
- Inhale deeply through your nose.
- Hold your breath and count to 5.
- Slowly release the air by exhaling through your nose.

EMBODYING AN ASSERTIVE STANCE

Maintain an assertive body posture that helps you feel more confident and empowered when entering a tense situation or difficult discussion. Maintain constant eye contact and a neutral look on your face.

TRY SOMEONE YOU KNOW AND TRUST

Try practising with a trusted friend to test alternative communication styles if you have an important issue to discuss. Say out loud what you feel like saying. Take note of how they respond to your tone of voice and body language. Ask yourself whether it is possible to communicate without being shy or hostile. Afterwards, evaluate the evidence. Modify your strategy in response to their feedback.

BELIEVE IN YOUR VALUE

Without a healthy and compassionate sense of self-worth, you will either choose to accept a request from others or end up offering more than you get. If you don't believe in yourself, how can you expect others to believe in you and give you what you want.

Establish Usable Boundaries

Remember that assertiveness and defiance are not the same thing. According to Ashleigh Edelstein (Marriage & Family Therapis LMFT), assertiveness is described as "being able to assert one's needs or requests politely and within personal boundaries."

Consider the following example if setting boundaries seems aggressive or awkward to you: your supervisor continually gives you tasks without asking if you are actually available to do them.

A violent reaction would be to yell at the supervisor in a meeting or to insist that someone else do the work.

An assertive approach, on the other hand, would be to schedule a meeting with your supervisor to consider a new method of distributing work, or to brainstorm different ways to properly divide tasks.

Start small by creating Practice Scenarios

If this all seems a bit overwhelming, start with some simple exercises to help you practice being more assertive in low-risk environments.

If you would rather stay home and watch a movie than go out, say so openly.

Inform your partner that you will not be able to complete a particular errand. This is also a great way to practice saying no without including a full backstory.

Go to a new restaurant and ask for a table by the window or somewhere quieter. And if no one is available, it remains a great opportunity to practice asking for what you want.

EVALUATE YOUR COMMUNICATION STYLE

The first step to being more assertive is to examine how you express your thoughts and emotions. Do you have a passive or active speaking style?

If you have a passive personality, you put the needs of others before your own. Although you may have good intentions, your speaking style will lead to negative frustration over time.

An aggressive personality, on the other hand, violates the rights of others and therefore being assertive is not the same as being aggressive. The assertive approach implies no threat, no coercion, but only the expression of your expectations or wishes.

If you are not sure which category you belong to, consider the following example.

A friend asks for a favour. You have helped this person many times and are fed up with it. Rather, you would like to devote your time to a personal project.
Depending on your communication style, here is how you might respond:

- Passive. *"Of course! I'd love to help you!"*
- Aggressive. *"I'm tired of your complaints and demands. You never do anything on your own."*
- Assertive. *"I can't help you this time."*

You have the habit of saying yes to something without bothering about it, I suggest you use some useful phrases for when you are faced with a proposal or invitation that you are not interested in.

Here are some ideas to get you started:

- *"I'll get back to you later."*
- *"I have various commitments."*
- *"I can't do that, I already have appointments."*
- *"I have to check my schedule."*

If you claim you have to double-check something, don't forget to reply to the person as soon as possible in the future.

Above all, bear in mind that you do not have to justify your decision regarding an appeal or invitation. If you feel guilty while trying to express yourself, remember that saying no to a request does not imply condemnation of the individual.

HOW TO INCREASE CONFIDENCE AND SELF-ESTEEM IN ASSERTIVE MANNER

When we have difficulty speaking up for ourselves and being assertive, we may feel stuck, vulnerable, or nervous.

Learning to talk openly about your wants and needs isn't easy for anyone.

Some people acquire these skills spontaneously, while others must struggle for several years to overcome feelings of embarrassment and remorse that prevent them from becoming assertive.

Assertiveness is one of the most powerful traits we can possess, both in our personal lives and at work.

If you are struggling to learn this skill, I have developed a series of activities that can help you.

In the same way that training works to develop physical strength, assertive listening exercises can help build your self-esteem.

Each individual learns differently and a technique that works for one person may not always work for another. Take the time to determine which is best for you.

I've collected some excellent examples of assertiveness training games and exercises to help you determine the best way to develop this skill:

1. UNDERSTAND YOUR HIERARCHY OF NEEDS.

Think of this exercise as an experiment in which you are both the researcher and the subject to be analyzed. As you collect data and become more informed, this feeling gives you a sense of power as the information is a source of control.

To become more assertive, you must first consider your desires. While it may be clear, you may find it difficult to recognize unmet needs right away.

To help you, you should employ Maslow's Hierarchy of Needs, a pyramid of human needs that each person can meet to live a happier life. This pyramid is a great place to start.

Take a few minutes to assess how much you put into meeting your needs at each step of the pyramid. Use this exercise to identify areas that would benefit from change.

2. VIEW YOUR WISHES

Visualization is an important method of mastering any skill. Figuring out what you want and seeing it with your mind's eye, or written on a whiteboard, is the first step to doing it.

Assertive people have a good understanding of their possibilities and can determine which paths are worth taking. When you visualize all your desires in an imaginary room, you can tell which ones are less important to you and which ones inspire you the most.

Paste photographs that reflect your aspirations, desires, and personal needs onto a poster board or online whiteboard.

These can be less important, such as your eating habits, or extremely important, such as how you prefer to handle a relationship.

This exercise allows you to practice prioritizing your wants and needs, choosing the most important to have on the board and in your life. This will help you recognize what is really important to you rather than what others think is.

3. CULTIVATE A NEW SPORT

One of the primary ways we express assertive behavior is through body language. Sports, dance, and other forms of physical activity such as Pilates and Yoga are excellent ways to reconnect with the body.

A confident individual is physically calm and their attitude puts people at ease, allowing them to build stronger relationships. When you feel calmer, you can speak more clearly and confidently.

Let's say basketball is your favorite sport. Asking to play a game at your nearest gym is a good way to practice asking for something that fits your sports needs while connecting with others.

4. CONTROL YOUR EMOTIONS

When practicing assertive actions, pay attention to emotional feedback.

- How did your boss' reaction make you feel when you asked for a pay raise?
- If they had said no, would it have been as horrible as you thought?
- Can you identify specific physical sensations and associate them with an emotion?

For the next few days, if you find yourself in situations that require assertive behavior, note what the circumstance was, whether you participated in a passive, agressive, or assertive activity, and what emotions accompanied you.

This will help you differentiate negative emotional reactions from circumstances in which you need to defend yourself.

5. KEEP A WRITTEN JOURNAL ABOUT ROLE-PLAYING GAMES

Consider two different situations each day and write a passive, passive-aggressive, aggressive, and assertive response for each.

For example, consider the following scenario: a colleague decided to switch shifts with you, but had to cancel at the last minute.

- An aggressive response would be, *"Find someone else to switch shifts with. I can't anymore."*
- *"Oh, all right,"* a passive person might say. *"Let's stay as we agreed. Don't worry about it."*
- "Fine," might be a passive-aggressive response. "Whatever. Do whatever you have to do." (sarcastically)
- An assertive response would be, *"When you canceled, it put me in a pretty tough position. I would appreciate it if you would let me know ahead of time whether or not you are able to cover for me."*

Jot down the negative emotions you might feel for each response, in all situations.

6. EMBODY YOUR EMOTIONS

This exercise will help you relate your thoughts to your body language. In a group of three or more people, have someone express an emotion exclusively through their body.

The other members of the group must guess which emotion they are embodying, and then take turns choosing another feeling and mimicking it.

As the rounds go by, it will be easier to identify feelings right away. This game will help you practice managing your physicality and sensing motivation even if you don't feel it.

When your body assumes a confident and assertive posture, your brain responds by releasing a sense of pride.

7. DO AN EXERCISE FOR ACTORS

This game is intended to help performers get used to listening to their scene partner rather than relying entirely on their lines or motivations. Being assertive, on the other hand, requires being attentive to the moods and feelings of others and listening consciously.

The goal of this game is to use different strategies to get your partner from one side of the room to the other.

You must first attempt to push them into the space using an offensive approach, then a defensive approach, and finally an assertive approach. When the other person feels they are being assertively questioned, they may choose to move.

8. SAY NO

To test your assertiveness, practice saying "no" firmly and getting "no" for an answer. Take turns with a friend in being the one asking the questions and the one getting the answers. For each round, the person answering "no" must state their answer firmly, and the questioner can then ask questions to ascertain why they answered that way.

This exercise is useful because it allows each participant to assertively request a need or request and practice being rejected. Immediately thereafter, one must strive to understand why the request was rejected, based on various reasons.

If the person who says "no" feels that the other party understood the explanation by modifying the request and tailoring it to the needs, the person who answered "no" can modify their response in the affirmative.

9. LOOK AT YOURSELF IN THE MIRROR

Step in front of a mirror for a few minutes. First, take note of how you're holding yourself and try to adjust your breathing. Keep an eye on your chest as it swells and deflates.
Do you feel calm or tense?
Visualize how the breath moves and how it is able to relieve anxiety.
After that, start an assertive conversation. Take note of how your body changes if you remain calm or nervous. Refocus your breathing after each sentence and try to maintain a calm posture.
Over time, you'll have more control over choosing a comfortable posture in intense situations.

10. THE POWER OF POSITIVE AFFIRMATIONS

One method of gaining someone's trust is through persuasion. Positive affirmations and mantras will help reformulate neural circuits in the brain, allowing you to unlearn unpleasant reactions to specific emotional circumstances.
A conscious language and positive thinking will lead you to express your full potential, opening the doors of your unconscious and making you live new experiences in your inner life and, as a result, in the outer one.

You will find that you are more receptive and find new solutions that you may not have thought of before.

Positive affirmations can be used at any time, by writing them on post-it notes around the house, in the office or on the desktop of your PC.

There are so many ways, what's important is that you don't forget to do it!

<u>CONCLUSION</u>

Assertive dialogue is essential for asserting one's rights and upholding one's limitations. It is synonymous with a variety of verbal and nonverbal characteristics and does not include offensive speech that denies the rights of others.

There are many standardized strategies for teaching assertiveness, such as SEL systems in schools and ways in which parents encourage assertive behaviors in their children.

It is helpful to take steps to become a more assertive communicator as assertive communication has been correlated with a variety of beneficial outcomes such as improved self-image, stronger partnerships, less anxiety, greater self-respect, and decreased disputes.

Assertive contact in the work sphere is often linked to a more fulfilling professional life.

Assertiveness on behalf of our neighbors and community members is also essential to building civic institutions in which all people are treated fairly, ethically, and compassionately.

As a society, we will achieve these goals by upholding the example of American civil rights leader John Lewis, who said, *"When you see something that is not fair, equitable or right, you must raise your voice. You have to say and do something.*

Assertiveness is therefore something that is not exclusively about ourselves; it is about raising our voices in favor of justice for all of humanity. If you would like to delve deeper into the concepts articulated in the book and feel ready for a coaching experience, visit my website:

www.coachingspace.it

I guarantee it will be my privilege and pleasure to teach and support you on this journey.

One moment, one last thing

If you enjoyed this book or found it useful, I would be very grateful if you would post a short review on Amazon. Your support makes all the difference and I personally read all reviews so I can get your feedback and make this book even better.

Thank you for your help !

Roberto Vingelli

AUTHOR.

CEO-Founder of the company Management Space, creator and owner of the brands "Coaching Space", "Gestioni Benessere" and "Life SPAce" with which I have provided consultancy and coaching to SPAs but also to structured companies in the beauty and wellness market.

Since 1989 in the sales and coaching sector, I have worked with multinational brands both Italian and foreign.
For the past 20 years, I have always held management and leadership roles.

Expert connoisseur of company dynamics, management and coordination of sales networks, recruitment, training, team building, great traveller.
Specialisations in Motivation, Personal Growth, Coaching, NLP, Hypnosis.

Passionate about psychology texts, couple dynamics, Italian Renaissance, Japanese and Zen culture, yoga and meditation, in continuous training and study because you never stop growing, learning and evolving.

I trained in Coaching with a master's degree and my course of study is in line with the 2015 UNI-11601 Standard - Recognised by AICP and approved by ICF.

My approach comes from Humanistic Evolutionary Coaching, based on Positive Psychology.

My holistic - relational sensibility goes to stimulate the deepest levers, relating to the axiom that the outer world reflects the inner world.

To change and improve, one must start with oneself. This, not only in personal and relational life but also in business life.

Printed in Great Britain
by Amazon

23244297R00099